balance the
BRIDGE

*Enhance your communication
skills and improve your life!*

BRAD MEISBURG

ISBN: 1494475413
ISBN 13: 9781494475413

This book is dedicated to my parents, Marion and Jack Meisburg. It was they who initially taught me the value of how you communicate with people…to use good manners, have respect for others, use teachings of the Bible and the Golden Rule, which basically sums up good communication: "Do unto others as you would have them do unto you."

Plus, their high expectations of me, and their sacrifices to send me to college, put me in a position to study, learn and grow daily in the understanding of this topic. Although my mother left this earth a number of years ago, I can only hope that she is proud of this book from heaven. I also hope this one will pass the test with Dad, as he is an amazing writer and teacher. Mother and Dad – thanks for all your love and support!

CONTENTS

PREFACE

The purpose of this book is to help the reader gain greater happiness in life. Many sources define happiness as a state of well-being and contentment. And there are countless opinions and discussions on what can bring about happiness. For many people, this can include deep relationships, strong religion, self-actualization, caring for others... and the list goes on and on. Much has been written about myths when it comes to happiness. One saying often repeated is "Money can't buy happiness". I happen to believe that... but I also believe in the saying "Lack of money can cause misery". Someone probably said that before me, but since I'm not sure, I'll take credit for that one.

This book will intend to convince the reader that a lack of communication skills can negatively impact one's life, often resulting in misery. And using a simple communications method can, in fact, have a very positive impact on one's life; often leading to happiness in many areas.

I am very thankful for the life I have lived so far. In fact, if I die tomorrow (which would be a relatively early age!), I certainly could not complain. I have been fortunate to live in the greatest country the world has ever seen and have had unbelievable opportunities throughout my life.

It has been through these opportunities that I have discovered the amazing importance of communication skills. And, how communication skills can enable so many things as we walk through almost every situation in life. Now it's my turn to share these concepts and a model that for some people could change their life. In other cases, there may be simply a nugget or two that the reader can use – my hope is that every reader finds something valuable. I can assure you that the best communicators use these concepts, and if you read on you can learn to use them also.

I would like to thank my wife, Betty, and my children, Ali and Jack, for putting up with me all of these years as I wrote this book. I know they grew tired of hearing me talk about it, and they probably thought that I would never actually finish it, as many other things took higher priority during the writing. Even I thought at times it would never actually get finished, yet here we are, and you are reading it, so mission accomplished!

INTRODUCTION

It was a beautiful morning at the Caneel Bay Resort on the island of St. John in the US Virgin Islands. We were taking a morning walk when just in front of us stood a deer, grazing gently. It was a buck, only four to six points on the antlers, still very young. He continued grazing as we continued to walk along the path. Apparently what he wanted to eat was very close to the path – maybe five feet from the edge. When we were only a few feet from him, he fixed his eyes on us but continued to graze. With no conversation, we were communicating that we were not threatening; and he was constantly validating this by watching our every move. It was the eyes of the deer that formed the bridge between us in this encounter. His eyes and our eyes were connected, or bridged. For that brief moment, the bridge seemed perfectly balanced. It was simple, but very powerful.

For over thirty years, I've been studying the way people communicate with each other. This fascination with communication began when, as a young electrical engineer, I made a decision to sell computers for a living.

In the early 1980s, a relatively small computer company named Hewlett Packard was hiring "Field Engineers." HP was primarily an electronic instrument company, but getting into the computer business was necessary because the instruments were getting so sophisticated that early computers were needed to control them and collect the kind of test data the instruments were able to produce. "Sales training" at that time was all about product knowledge.

Bill Hewlett and Dave Packard were strong believers in the "next bench" syndrome. This was a simple concept about making the best product on the market for engineers. When an engineer in a lab had a new HP product on his bench, the engineer on the "next bench" would want one also. Although I was a bit concerned about a new career in sales, Kerry Roller, who would be my new manager and a very talented sales manager, convinced me that the "next bench" focus would keep me technical, and thus my young career began. I quickly learned that there was more to selling than having good product knowledge, and remaining technical became the least of my worries.

Senior sales people in our field office talked about the importance of building relationships and the value of developing excellent communication skills. I witnessed key examples of this when we won the sale, and also disastrous scenarios when we were beaten badly by our competition. Often the company winning the business did not have the best product or solution, but in fact did the best job of bridging their proposal to the customer's problem. My realization of the importance of a communication "bridge" began.

I discovered that selling was not just about having a good pitch on your product or service – it was about the ability to establish in the customer's mind that you really understood their problem and that you could best solve that problem. Using a two-way communication bridge was critical. Therefore, I soon recognized that the customer's communication skills are a variable in a selling situation. I began to think of every conversation as a bridge where the flow of traffic both ways is critical for the sales person *and* the customer to get where they want to go. Without reasonable flow of traffic in both directions, the bridge is inefficient – essentially "unbalanced." Thus, the concept of Balance the Bridge was born.

> In order to gain complete understanding of a customer problem, you not only need to understand their company and their industry, but you also must create a communication bridge that has two-way traffic.

There are hundreds of books and courses on improving communication skills. I've read many and been certified to teach some. What's different about this one? I've developed a simple model that is easy to understand and puts focus not only on the sender, but also on the receiver and on the bridge that must exist. This model covers many different types of communication situations – not just one on one. Through successful examples you'll be able to see how others have mastered these skills, and by the end of the book you'll learn the importance of balance, not only in business communication, but also in many areas of life. The concepts described in this book might help you have a long, successful marriage and a positive relationship with your relatives and friends.

My degree as an Electrical Engineer did not include Communications Theory, but over 30 years of experience in business have taught me what works and what does not work as we attempt to balance the bridges of communication.

Balance the Bridge is about thinking of the simple task of holding a conversation and understanding what is really going on from a process perspective. It's about break-

> Balance the Bridge is about the ability to practice what I call *communications process excellence*.

ing the code on why certain relationships don't work well, or why organizations struggle even when it appears they are set up for success.

Who can benefit by reading this book?

- Individuals who want to advance their careers
- Business leaders who want a more effective team
- Companies striving to be more successful and gain higher customer satisfaction
- People who want to be more valuable to the groups or organizations they associate with
- Anyone who is involved in a challenging relationship
- Parents who want a better relationship with their children
- People who want a better relationship with their spouse or significant other

Sound like a large target audience? Absolutely.

Try to think of someone who doesn't need to communicate.

I have been in the private sector for over 30 years in both leadership and individual contributor positions. I have been fortunate to work for a very successful company, Hewlett Packard, and I learned from the leadership of the founders, Bill Hewlett and Dave Packard. Most of my career has been in direct customer facing activities such as sales and consulting, but I also have led teams in marketing and industry solution strategy, planning and operations. In fact, operational excellence for field professionals has become my specialty, including process improvement to track and analyze results.

During the 1990s, I led a consulting organization at HP of about 350 people. We delivered sales support and technology infrastructure consulting to about 25% of our large US clients at that time, using our own resources and a number of partners. In a four-year period we took this part of the business from $15M to $80M in revenue while exceeding profit targets.

At one point I noticed that our leadership team, reporting to me, was not functioning well as a team. They all had individual success with their respective teams, but we didn't function well as a senior leadership team. Overall results were good, but I envisioned much greater performance if we had a senior team that worked well together. A manager on my staff suggested the use of an outside consultant. Originally I was skeptical, but it turned out to be the best decision we ever made. The consultant began by simply observing how we worked together on everything from impromptu meetings to formal business reviews. The findings were fascinating. We spent much too much time "advocating" our positions. Very few people were listening. Listening was really "waiting to talk." We had no real guiding principles for interaction. The loudest person often was the one to assume control of the dialogue.

Once we recognized the problems and took the advice of the consultant, communications improved. We were more productive, and people were much happier to work on our team. Terms like "appreciative inquiry" and "consciously extending meeting topics" became part of the way that we did business.

We were ruthless about having a timekeeper, facilitator and scribe at every meeting. These people could not be content providers in the meetings unless they asked to step out of their role. In short, we became a high performing leadership team, and I began to establish the belief that the bridges formed between people who are trying to communicate are often weak or even non-existent. It's like looking across the Grand Canyon and not being able to get to the other side. However, when the bridge is formed and becomes properly balanced, efficiency, productivity and satisfaction can explode.

A few years ago I was asked to create and assemble the dashboard of the Enterprise Business Group, which was approximately one-third of HP – over $30B in revenue.

A "dashboard" in this case is a document that shows results against key metrics, and most importantly the trending of results. Operational excellence, in this case, is about tracking the right qualitative and quantitative data points and trends in order to achieve the business goals set in the plan, be it an annual plan or a longer-term strategic plan.

Operational excellence is also about defining key standard processes in order to improve efficiency and replicate best practices. The dashboard became the vehicle for strategic conversations at the CEO level. It was only effective if there was a good balance of information that could lead to a quick understanding of the key metrics and lead to quick decisions in a very complex environment.

I've applied these process concepts to the critical art of communication in order to help you identify ways to improve and get better results from conversations.

If all of your friends, relatives and co-workers tell you that you have totally mastered the art of communication, give this book to someone who needs it. If not, read on!

Brad Meisburg
January 2014

Chapter 1

THE BRIDGE AS A COMMUNICATION MODEL

The term "bridge" is often defined as a structure spanning and providing passage over a gap or barrier. There are millions of natural and man-made bridges in the world. I've always been fascinated with bridges, and with how many of the man-made bridges have become famous icons for a city or region. A great example is the Golden Gate Bridge in San Francisco – one of my favorites. When it was completed in 1937, it instantly became the longest suspension bridge span in the world, and it is certainly an internationally recognized symbol of San Francisco and the United States. Along with standing as an engineering marvel and facilitating travel between the city of San Francisco and Marin County, it also has the distinction of being considered the most popular place to commit suicide in the world![1] That's certainly not a positive attribute, but is, nevertheless, an indication of the attention and fascination that comes with bridges.

---

[1] Bone, James (2008-10-13). "The Times" (ECE). New York. Retrieved 2010 – 11 - 15

THE GOLDEN GATE BRIDGE

FLAWED BRIDGES

The U.S. Bureau of Transportation Statistics estimates the number of bridges in the U.S. to be over 600,000 - not including railroad bridges. Some studies have found that 25% of these bridges are either structurally deficient or functionally obsolete. That simple statistic should give you pause the next time you drive over a bridge. Are you on one that is on that list? A few years ago, the I-35W Bridge collapsed in Minneapolis, killing 13 people and injuring 100 more. My guess is that none of those people thought the bridge might collapse as they were driving across it. The stability of our infrastructure is something that we take for granted. Bridges are supposed to be like water, food and electricity – always available and in good condition for our use. However, our infrastructure is not always stable.

Like physical bridges, communication bridges are not necessarily stable or constant. However, repairing communication bridges can be much less expensive by following a simple process.

> The good news is that unlike the high cost to repair 150,000 bridges in the U.S., communication bridges can be developed or repaired at a relatively low cost. Once you understand the principles, it is a simple matter of following a series of steps designed to make sure a stable communication bridge exists during the conversation.

BALANCED BRIDGES

Just as traffic engineers work to balance the flow of traffic across a bridge, effective communicators learn to balance conversations, making adjustments when necessary. When you can identify the most appropriate type of communication and adjust the balance between you and the other person, you can set up the best possible

---

Are you in "poor communication denial"?
Millions of people make communication mistakes every day because they don't think about their conversations. They know they make mistakes, but they don't want to change. They are in "poor communication denial." The first step is to admit that you need to, and want to, improve your communication skills. A good example is the person who knows they talk too much, but does nothing to improve.

---

bridge and achieve your desired outcome. You may want to demonstrate good manners, or just be friendly by saying "hello" to someone. Or you may be discussing a complicated business proposal. Sadly, people every day make simple communication mistakes, reducing the chances of the desired outcome.

Because communication relationships vary, we need to be able to construct an appropriate bridge and balance for each interaction. In the next chapters, we'll examine various types of relationships and strategies for constructing workable bridges.

Over many years I have simplified the process to include 5 simple steps. You will find the process easy to learn and remember, which should allow you to use it for every conversation, until the steps become simply part of the way you communicate.

Let's examine the 5 steps:

Step 1 – Recognize the Relationship and Situation

Relationships between people can vary from very simple or very complex. Simplifying relationships into a few categories will allow you to create the best bridge possible and to determine how the bridge should operate.

At the same time you recognize the relationship, you must also recognize the situation. It may be a conversation with just one other person or there may be multiple people involved. Recognizing the situation ensures that the nature of the conversation will be appropriate.

Step 2 – Imagine the Bridge

This step in the process keeps you from heading in the wrong direction. When you drive a car, you are taught to start the engine, put your foot on the brake, put the car into gear and look both ways before you start moving. Imagining the bridge forces you to think and visualize before you begin talking.

Step 3 – Establish and Anchor the Bridge

When you begin the conversation, you take the necessary steps to make sure both sides of the bridge are connected and secure—just as engineers do when building a physical bridge.

Step 4 – Manage the Traffic

Physical bridges have traffic lanes and signs to keep cars moving and to prevent accidents. Sometimes flashing lights and tolls are used. Skilled communicators create "verbal lanes and signs" that manage the flow of conversation so that both parties can communicate effectively, and ultimately achieve the communication goal or objective.

Step 5 – Close the Bridge

Many communication bridges have been effectively established but then destroyed because they were closed too early, closed inappropriately, or not closed at all.

For the skilled communicator, these steps happen in seconds when the conversation is short. Anyone who plays the game of golf knows that a golf swing lasts no more than a second or two, but when you are taught how to swing a golf club; the instructor breaks down the swing into a series of steps. First you address the ball in the appropriate stance, followed by a smooth take away, an appropriate backswing followed by a downswing with hip rotation, strike the ball squarely and finally a good follow through.

> Communications is like the game of golf – we need to learn the steps and practice them over and over until they become second nature.

Once you know the steps, you must practice them over and over until they become second nature and the golf swing becomes a smooth process of all steps with really no break between any step.

Similarly, with the right amount of practice, using the proper steps, anyone can become a skilled communicator.

If there is any great secret of success in life, it lies in the ability to put yourself in the other person's place and to see things from his point of view – as well as your own.
Henry Ford

Chapter 2

THE FIRST STEP: RECOGNIZE THE RELATIONSHIP AND SITUATION

At the beginning of each chapter I will introduce an interesting bridge from somewhere in the world. By the end of the book I hope that you will have learned about many of the wonderful bridges that have been built throughout history. I also hope this will help you internalize how a bridge and the flow of traffic can be used as a communication model. Just like physical bridges, you will learn that communication bridges can take on unique attributes.

The ancient Romans built the first large and lasting bridges.[2] Many of these are still standing today. A great example is the Alcantara Bridge in Spain. This Roman stone arch bridge was built over the Tagus River at Alcantara, Spain, between 104 and 106 AD by an order of the Roman Emperor Trajan in 98[3]. The damage to this

---

[2] O'Connor, Colin (1993), *Roman Bridges*, Cambridge University Press, ISBN 0-521-39326-4

[3] Whitney, Charles S. (2003) [1929], *Bridges of the World: Their Design and Construction*, Mineola, New York: Dover Publications, pp. 75–79, ISBN 0-486-42995-4

bridge over the years has been greater from war than from the elements. The Romans used well-defined processes and engineering to build bridges that would serve the desired purpose and stand the test of time.

THE ALCANTARA BRIDGE

© Can Stock Photo Inc. / Marzolino

The ancient Romans taught us that a well thought out process could be used to build outstanding physical bridges. In similar fashion, the creation of a communication "bridge" requires a well thought out process.

Understanding the relationship between yourself and the person with whom you want to communicate is critical. Sometimes this understanding is simple and quick; at other times it's complex and time consuming.

For the purpose of this model, we will classify relationships into two basic categories:

1) Peer-to-peer

2) Subordinate-to-position of authority

In a peer-to-peer relationship, both parties are equals. Think of two good friends, a husband and wife, or college roommates. The key aspect of peer-to-peer is that no one is "in control." Communication is an equal exchange between equal individuals. In the subordinate-to-position of authority relationship, one person has power over the other. Think of a military drill sergeant talking to a private, a mother talking to her two year old child, or a boss giving specific directions to an employee. Good communicators distinguish themselves by correctly identifying the various relationships they find themselves in every day. However, a common problem is that some people don't know how to recognize the relationship, and/or *who they are* in the relationship. Often the employee having the conversation with the boss is behaving as if it's a

> Early in life, I received this advice from my father. . .
>
> "No one ever **listened** himself out of a job."
>
> The unfortunate corollary:
>
> Every day someone **talks** himself out of a job.

peer- to-peer relationship. Although these types of conversations certainly can occur, it's a highly desirable skill to know **when** the relationship moves from one person having authority over the other to both people being "equal" in the relationship. In most work situations, you must earn the trust of the authority over time to have a peer-to-peer dialogue. You also have to exhibit sensitivity to the reality that at any moment the conversation can turn back to the position of authority and subordinate.

In the peer-to-peer relationship, a reasonable goal is to have an even exchange, with both parties talking and listening equally. In a position of authority relationship, the boss always has the option of giving direction, and if you are the subordinate, you

> *The subordinate's goal is to be able to identify quickly whether the relationship at any given moment is peer-to-peer or subordinate to position of authority.*

must yield to this direction. Stay alert because the level of traffic may change suddenly to peer-to-peer. The conservative approach for the subordinate is to listen and ask clarifying questions while avoiding strong expressions of opinions unless invited to do so. In some environments, however, listening and never expressing any opinions may be viewed as a lack of assertiveness.

An example:

The president of a textbook company, at a meeting with sales managers to discuss how to cut costs and increase sales, asks them for opinions on why the new math textbook isn't meeting sales expectations. One of the managers responds that many states have changed the way math is being taught. The president seems interested in the response and asks follow-up questions. Another manager, thinking the president is open for solutions, suggests that the textbook be rewritten to match the new methods of instruction. The president responds that a rewrite would be too costly and take too much time. The solution for increasing sales will have to be budget neutral. The sales manager is confused and frustrated. He responds that he thought the president wanted possible solutions, and he's sure a rewrite will solve the problem. The president cuts him off with, "Didn't you hear what I just said?"

Communication diagnosis: The president switched quickly to position of authority when a high cost solution was proposed. The sales manager missed the switch.

In defining the situation, we will classify the number of bridges to be balanced.

Single Bridge Situation vs. Multiple Bridge Situation

In a single bridge situation there is a one-to-one dialogue. If more than two people are in the discussion, the situation moves to multiple bridges. I generally categorize the multiple bridge situation as either "one-to-few" or "one-to-many". The situation can, in fact, become much more complicated than this. However, these two categories of multiple bridge situations will enable you to navigate the majority of communication scenarios.

Imagine that you are having lunch with two friends. You have two peer-to-peer bridges to build and manage—a "one-to-few" situation. Communication mistakes happen frequently in "one-to-few" situations when one person is left out of the conversation, with no attempt made to bring them into the dialogue. In a "one-to-many" situation, you must manage bridges and traffic to everyone who is listening. If you are giving a presentation (speech, sermon, etc.) to a room full of people, most of the traffic actually flows from you to them. Therefore, skills are needed to keep your audience engaged and interested. We'll examine these in greater detail in the chapter on Case Studies.

As soon as we identify the relationship and situation, we have to quickly assess if there are other variables.

Are moods or emotions part of the conversation?

Perhaps you are going to have a chat with your best friend. Right away you may be able to sense if your friend seems quite normal, or sad, or upset. Sensitivity to the other person's mood is critical. We often greet people with a "How are you?" but do we *really listen to the answer?* A great technique is to ask another open-ended question after the answer rather than launching into your story. I find that most mistakes made in this area are made by "selfish communicators." These are the people who monopolize conversations by talking about their life, their troubles, their family, their job, their hobbies and on and on. They often seem oblivious to the fact that they communicate in this manner.

Do you know people like this? If so, give them this book as they can benefit from these concepts. (Better yet, send them to balancethebridge.com so that they can buy their own copy!... pardon the shameless plug.) Of course, it's quite normal to want to share "our" life in conversations. However, you'll find greater success and happiness if you strive for balanced conversations. In fact, people who have mastered the skill often find that other people are more interested in them and their life once they stop trying to constantly dominate conversations.

More on the Multiple Bridge Situation

As I mentioned, if more than two people are involved in the conversation the situation involves multiple bridges. Let's look at a few examples:

We discussed the situation where you might be having lunch with 2 friends – a "one-to-few" situation. A "one-to-many" situation example would be if you were communicating to a group of your peers—perhaps delivering a presentation at a neighborhood meeting. The goal is to get your message across and achieve your objective. Do you simply want people to understand an update on some topic or are you trying to convince the group to accept a concept and agree to take action? The most frequent mistakes in this situation are a) not testing for understanding and b) failing to have a well thought out objective.

Picture a staff meeting of four people: the boss and three subordinates. This is a "one-to-few" situation. The boss has to be careful to retain the position of authority and, at the same time, make sure that all four people are engaged in the meeting. A classic challenge in this situation is dealing with one subordinate who tries to dominate the meeting. We'll discuss the best ways to deal with this situation in the chapter on case studies.

Good examples of the "one-to-many" situation include a CEO of a company delivering a speech to 100 employees or when a teacher explains a chemistry formula in front of 30 students. Understanding how the communication should flow is critical for success. In the example of the CEO addressing 100 employees, the

CEO is obviously in a position of authority. However, the CEO also must inform and motivate the employees in order to drive success for the company. The best CEOs know how to make sure that the message is getting through – essentially an "anchored" bridge during the communications. The ability to take questions from the employees is one method of balancing the flow of traffic, or at least a demonstration that the CEO is willing to listen and answer questions or address concerns. Some best practices for people in a position of authority to enable two-way traffic across the bridge include:

- Allow a significant amount of time for Q&A, including a facilitator who can start the Q&A with some pre-submitted questions.
- Avoid criticizing suggestions or questions.
- Once you answer a question, check to make sure that the person asking understood the answer.
- Offer multiple ways for questions to be asked, including e-mail, web site forms, etc.

REVIEW: RELATIONSHIPS AND SITUATIONS

Relationship	Situation	Example
Peer-to-Peer	One-to-One	Two friends talking
Peer-to-Peer	One-to-Few	Four friends having lunch
Peer-to-Peer	One-to-Many	Committee member presenting to large committee of equals
Position of Authority	One-to-One	Boss and employee
Position of Authority	One-to-Few	Drill Sergeant with three Privates
Position of Authority	One-to-Many	CEO of a company addressing 300 employees

Chapter 3

IMAGINE THE BRIDGE: A VISUAL MODEL

Among the many beautiful bridges in Asia would certainly be the Si-o-Seh Pol located in Isfahan, Iran. Si-o-Seh Pol actually means the Bridge of 33 Arches. The Persians learned the use of stable arches from the Romans, and this bridge was built around 1600 A.D. under the order of Shah Abbas I. Roughly 300 meters in length, this bridge is a double deck arch bridge, allowing pedestrians to walk across and enjoy the view of the river and the city.

When you begin to imagine the bridge, it's a good idea to pick an appropriate bridge of beauty. After all, most conversations should be enjoyable!

SI-O-SEH POL

© Can Stock Photo Inc. / shanin

The Communications Bridge is a mental model that you must understand and adopt in order to take advantage of this philosophy. Think of your favorite bridge either from seeing it in person or in a photo or video. Perhaps this is a bridge in a city you have visited or one that you cross daily in your hometown. The bridge is in place to allow people to get from one side to the other. There is traffic in both directions. Some bridges are busy 24 hours a day, 7 days a week … remote bridges over streams can be quiet with no traffic for days. Nevertheless, the ability for traffic to get from one side to the other is the purpose of the bridge.

Now, think of a conversation with someone you find very easy to talk to. As soon as you encounter the person, either face to face or over the phone, a conversation begins. It could be as simple as a two second "hello" or a conversation that lasts for hours. Now, imagine a bridge between the two of you...connected. The connected part is very important.

The words are the traffic going from one person's mouth to the other person's ears. And part of the communications, or traffic,

> A bridge not connected on both sides is worthless.

can be non-verbal. It could be the way the other person looks at you. It could be the pace of their speech or the tone of their voice. In any event, imagine the spoken words as traffic.

Thinking of your example, try answering the following questions:

1) Is the bridge anchored well on both sides?
2) Is traffic flowing both ways?
3) At the end of the conversation, did the experience feel well balanced?

The answer may not always need to be "yes" to the above questions, and we'll examine good reasons for this. However, in many cases, we do want all of the answers to be yes. "Yes to all 3 questions" can mean that both people feel good about the conversation. "Yes to all 3 questions" can mean that you'll get a chance to talk to this person again. "No to any of the 3 questions" could mean the beginning of a problem in a relationship, or that you're failing to convey and make your point. In some cases, it could mean the end of a relationship.

If I'm talking to you and you're not listening, the bridge is not anchored on your side. If I'm listening to you talk, but I never get a chance to say anything, the traffic is not flowing both ways. If both parties feel at the end of the conversation that it was "balanced," then the total volume of traffic flowing both ways was right. But if one party feels that things were not balanced, we need to examine the traffic pattern.

Think of a person who you know who has great communication skills. Think of the typical conversations you have with him or her. What are the characteristics of those conversations? Many people answer this with something like "he is a very good listener"… or "she is very easy to talk to"… or "I'm just at ease with her." This person may be very well trained or may just have the natural ability to create a balanced bridge between the two of you that seems comfortable. However, this kind of situation, although common, is not always balanced. If you're someone who talks constantly and has poor listening skills, the other person may simply be tolerating the situation. He or she may tell others that you are hard to talk to and you never listen. They may think the bridge is always unbalanced when they encounter you. In a later chapter I'll explain how to test whether your perception is the same as the other person's. I can't emphasize enough the importance of this initial imagery. Imagining the bridge first, then moving to the next step allows you to see your conversations in a totally different light.

> Developing your "bridge building" skills means taking a hard look at how you communicate today.

Chapter 4

ESTABLISH AND ANCHOR THE BRIDGE

The Bosphorus Bridge is unique in that it is today one of two bridges that connects Europe to Asia in Istanbul, Turkey. As of the time of this writing, there is yet a third bridge under construction across the Bosphorus Strait, which is very controversial, but the Turkish government continues to build the $2.5B structure.

You may find the need to build multiple bridges during a conversation, especially if the conversation involves multiple people.

The Bosphorus Bridge was built in the early 1970s and is a gravity anchored suspension bridge approximately one mile long. It is estimated that 200,000 vehicles pass daily in both directions. Now that's a lot of traffic to manage!

THE BOSPHORUS BRIDGE

© Can Stock Photo Inc. / DeReGe

Often communications fail in the first few seconds when they get off to a bad start. The best communicators know how to begin a conversation. In Balance the Bridge, I refer to this as establishing and anchoring the bridge.

> The most important part of this step is to quickly recognize not only the relationship, but also the mood or situation of the other person or people in the conversation.

It may seem simple, but the first thing you say is critical. Perhaps it is "Hello, how are you?"

The answer to this question is often a very short answer such as "fine, and you?" At this point, your answer and your next response can often tell you how best to proceed. Many skilled communicators will then reply with a short answer and ask another open ended question so that they can assess the situation. In this exchange, the skilled communicator is trying to anchor the bridge on both sides. Eye contact and body language become tools used to establish the anchors. Once the bridge is established it becomes time to manage the traffic.

However, you can't manage the traffic unless the bridge is established. It would be as if traffic were allowed on a bridge that was not yet completed...if a bridge is not complete, there is no safe way to get to the other side. Therefore, it becomes critical to establish the anchored bridge. The easy part for the skilled communicator is to have the bridge anchored on his or her side. Again, using eye contact, body language and open-ended questions can demonstrate that the bridge is firmly anchored and ready for traffic (words) coming to you. But making sure the bridge is anchored on the other side may not be so easy.

Let's take the example of communicating with the person who doesn't listen well. An open ended question may simply open the door for this type of person to talk for the next 30 minutes without ever taking a breath or demonstrating the desire to hear anything anyone else might say. In this example, the skilled communicator can interject with something like: ... "that story is very interesting...would you mind if I share something similar with you?" Essentially this is a request to talk, and will often cause those who talk too much to actually listen because they are not used to being asked that type of question...It can take the person by surprise. A critical part of this step is the action you take to get the bridge anchored on both sides before you try to let all traffic move back and forth. Plus if the bridge starts to fall apart on either side, you as the road crew must step back in and get it anchored again! Assuming we have solid anchors, it's time for traffic to flow...

Chapter 5

MANAGE THE TRAFFIC

When you talk about busy bridges, you can't leave out the George Washington Bridge that connects New Jersey and New York in the United States. This bridge was built in the late 1920s and opened in 1931. It is a double-decked suspension bridge crossing the Hudson River. Although recently the traffic volume has fluctuated with a controversial increase in the toll, the bridge averages close to 300,000 vehicles in total daily, which means the annual traffic can exceed 100 million vehicles.

Now, that said, if we are going to consider all types of traffic, you have to mention the Howrah Bridge in Kolkata, India. In addition to 80,000 vehicles per day, there are as many as 1 million pedestrians each day that cross the bridge…and that number does not include the cows!

Once you establish the communications bridge you must be prepared to manage the volume of traffic, which in some situations can be large and complex.

THE GEORGE WASHINGTON BRIDGE

© CAN STOCK PHOTO INC. / SEANPAVONEPHOTO

THE HOWRAH BRIDGE

© CAN STOCK PHOTO INC. / JOHNNYDEVIL

I hate traffic jams… we live north of Atlanta in a not so small town called Alpharetta, GA. Alpharetta used to be a small dairy community but the growth period of the last 30 years transformed Alpharetta from farmland to a busy suburb with serious traffic. And, of course, all of metro Atlanta is known for it's traffic challenges. You must choose the right time of day to travel or expect that it could take quite some time to go even 10 miles in any direction. I've been all over the world and witnessed tough traffic – Los Angeles, Washington, DC, New York City, Rome, London, Paris, Bangalore to name a few cities that have traffic challenges. In some cases, the infrastructure of the city is actually well designed and traffic jams are simply a result of too many cars. In the case of Atlanta, not only do we have too many cars, but we also have an infrastructure that was never designed to deal with as many people as actually live and work here. Managing large volumes of communication traffic can be challenging, but if you practice this step you can become very skilled at keeping the conversation moving at the right pace and volume.

In the first three steps of the process, you actually "build the infrastructure" which prepares for the conversation to occur. Then traffic may flow and if you have built the infrastructure correctly it becomes much easier to manage the traffic. Traffic management means the right level of talking and listening by each party. It does not necessarily mean that both parties spend the same amount of time talking but that at least there is a conscious decision on the balance.

The effective communicator measures the balance of traffic during the conversation and adjusts the flow as needed to achieve the appropriate balance. If the balance is about right, then no intervention is needed – however, let's take the example where the other person is not saying much of anything at all. Now is the time to ask some open-ended questions in order to generate more traffic coming from the quiet person. Another widely used technique in this situation is to check for understanding once you have made a point. Simply asking the question, "Does this make sense to you?" is generally a good way to not only get the other person to speak but often they will say more than a simple yes or no...especially if you pause and allow space for them to begin talking.

Sense when silence is a golden opportunity to allow the other person to talk. A pause for reflection can be very powerful, especially when giving a presentation to a group. If one tries to eat a good meal too fast, it can become an unpleasant experience. Conversations can be very much the same. Allow the conversation some time to digest on both sides. This sometimes is only a matter of seconds, yet a very important part of managing the communications traffic.

Now let's take the example of the person who simply won't stop talking – it's like you are drinking from a fire hose. When discussing communication skills with people, I most often hear about this type of person. In most cases, their message would be much more powerful if they simply said fewer words and would pause periodically to allow for reasonable traffic. This can be one of the most difficult challenges for the experienced communicator to deal with. The type of person who talks too much often is just focused on their situation, their problems, their family, their interests, etc. and they may not even really care to hear what you have to say. They may also be nervous and fearful of letting gaps appear in the conversation.

First of all, one of your key challenges is to make sure that you are not one of these people! We'll discuss how to do just that later in the chapter on Applying the Model. However, assuming you are not one of these people, and assuming you are having a conversation with someone who has this problem, you then need to use some techniques to establish some balance. Asking permission to speak sometimes will work with this type of person. Good examples are: May I tell you a short story about my situation?... or, Can I share with you a challenge I am having?

The endless talker is often not used to hearing something like this, and may be surprised and suddenly interested to hear what you have to say. In other cases, you might get ten seconds into your story and then they are off to the races again on something they want to tell you. If this is the case, you may need to get more direct...a possible response when you are interrupted might be "Can I please finish?"...

During the 2010 mid-term elections a few years ago in the U.S. and leading up to the elections there were many debates. This was a major opportunity to observe people who would not let the other person finish speaking before they would interrupt. As a matter of fact, interrupting people has become so common that it is expected when you turn on the TV.

Just try to watch shows like "The View" and count the number of times someone is interrupted. It's a sad display of rudeness that has become commonplace. In fact, that particular show has done well in the ratings over the years, which tells us that in general we have grown to accept this style of communication as normal and acceptable. In other words, many people don't even recognize that there is a problem. The person who is the loudest and most aggressive is often the person who is heard.

What is lost here is the fact that this behavior typically will not produce the most successful communication outcomes or the most meaningful relationships. The person who constantly interrupts is demonstrating the lack of care or concern for the other person. And, in the end, this type of behavior normally leads to many other types of problems throughout life.

Finally, you must learn to manage the traffic so that everyone is satisfied with the level of exchange of information. This can be tested in our final step of the process.

Chapter 6

CLOSE THE BRIDGE

In South America, the Octavio Frias de Oliveria Bridge was opened in 2008 with a construction cost that exceeded $450M. This cable-stayed bridge in Sao Paulo, Brazil over the Pinheiros River is unique in that it is the only bridge in the world that has two curved tracks supported by only one concrete mask. [4]

LED lighting of the bridge uses more than 50% less energy than traditional lighting.

Perhaps bridges to be built in the future can learn from the past plus use current technology to continue to improve them. Certainly this is my hope as we face the fact that many of our current bridges are in bad need of repair and reconstruction.

At times, older physical bridges are closed and newer, more efficient designs are constructed to replace them. Skilled communicators take advantage of new communication bridges that can be used. Great examples of these are social media platforms like LinkedIn, Twitter and Facebook.

---

[4] https://sites.google.com/site/octaviofriasdeoliveirabridge/, Retrieved 10-14-2013, https://sites.google.com/site/octaviofriasdeoliveirabridge/studio

In this chapter, we'll learn about the closing of a communication bridge at the end of each conversation, and why it's a critical step in the process.

THE OCTAVIO FRIAS DE OLIVERIA BRIDGE

© CAN STOCK PHOTO INC. / CELSODINIZUSA

All too often, I see people ending a conversation abruptly, leaving the other party feeling as if something was started but never finished appropriately. When a bridge is to be closed, there is an orderly process for gradually reducing the traffic in both directions, allowing everyone to safely get to the other side before the bridge is closed. Certainly there are times when there must be extremely quick conversations and interruptions; however, when possible a conversation that closes smoothly proves to be the most effective type of conversation.

If you are having a business conversation with someone, a smooth close is often a summary of what has been discussed and the next steps or actions. A parent having a conversation with a child perhaps could simply use a phrase such as "Do you understand?" to check for understanding. Someone chatting with a friend might simply say "It was great to see you, let's get together again soon, OK?"

There are hundreds or even thousands of possibilities here – the important concept is making sure that you understand the importance of a smooth close to the conversation, and leaving the bridge in good condition so that it is easily re-opened later.

Also, an effective closing can make sure that next steps are clear or that key points were understood. In selling, there is a specific type of conversation called "the close". Essentially this is a technique or skill designed to "close the sale" and win the deal. The most common mistake in closing business conversations is a lack of discussion and agreement on the next steps or actions required. Although this is somewhat of a simple step, it is critical in that this step can often dictate how or if future conversations will occur. Closing the bridge effectively can mean that both parties agree to the next conversation, and a summary of what was discussed can be very effective here.

Later in the book, we will discuss pitfalls and things that can go wrong in conversations. Over the last 20 years, I have specifically noticed that the rise in the amount of information coming at everyone has created an atmosphere where it is increasingly more difficult to keep track of what I will call "next steps". Conversations often are just for passing time with no real action, but much of the time there is specific action desired by at least one of the parties in the conversation.

Spending more focus on closing the bridge can positively affect this relatively recent trend. This will be discussed in greater detail in the sections on Case Studies and Developing the Action Plan.

What we've covered so far is an introduction to the use of the bridge metaphor in the development of effective communication skills and how it is used. Now, we'll specifically look at how you can apply the model and multiple examples to help you internalize why it works so well.

SUMMARY

Step 1 – Understand the Relationship and Situation

- Is the relationship Peer-to-Peer or Position of Authority?
- Is there one bridge to balance or multiple bridges?

Step 2 – Imagine the Bridge

- Use appropriate visual imagery and introductory comments depending on the relationship and situation

Step 3 – Establish and Anchor the Bridge

- Begin the conversation to set up appropriate bridges

Step 4 – Manage the Traffic

- Be sensitive to the flow patterns and adjust to keep the conversation appropriately balanced

Step 5 – Close the Bridge

- Avoid abrupt endings – close the conversation gracefully – test for success if appropriate

> *Give every man thy ear, but few thy voice.*
> *William Shakespeare*

Chapter 7

APPLYING THE MODEL

One of the most famous bridges in the world is the Tower Bridge in London, which crosses the river Thames. This bridge is a combination drawbridge and suspension bridge with two towers connected together at the upper level by two horizontal walkways. Often this bridge is mistakenly called the London Bridge, which is actually the next bridge upstream. Similar to the Golden Gate Bridge being seen as a symbol of San Francisco, the Tower Bridge is known as an iconic symbol of London.[5]

Properly constructed and maintained bridges can last a very long time. As you learn to apply the model, you will find that if a strong communication bridge is built early in a relationship, it can be maintained and function well for a very long time.

---

[5] www.earthinpictures.com, Retrieved 08-02-2011, http://www.earthinpictures.com/world/great_britain/london/tower_bridge.html

THE TOWER BRIDGE

© Can Stock Photo Inc. / sborisov

Now that you understand the model, it's time to discuss ways to apply it. And, depending on how skilled you already are in communicating with others, you will apply the model at a different pace. In general, you should:

1) Learn to observe conversations.

Instead of simply having dialogue throughout the day with your normal contacts, approach each situation with the intent of observing what is going on…. watch the way other people talk to each other. Try to determine if a bridge exists, if it is anchored on both sides, if traffic is moving appropriately for the relationship, etc. This is a critical first step so that you learn to observe the characteristics of an interaction, both positive and negative.

And, when observing conversations, try to pick situations where the dialogue will be predictably good and also situations where you think it will most likely be not so good… in this manner, you can watch the skilled and the un-skilled. Obviously, your goal is to become one of the skilled, improve your skills, or verify that you are skilled.

Begin to make a scorecard of conversations you observe and why they did or did not they seem to work well relative to the model. A sample Conversation Scorecard is located in the back of the book, or you can send an e-mail request to bmeisburg@balancethebridge. com to get a free sample. The Conversation Scorecard will allow you to use real life situations that occur each day as case studies. The good news is that you can see a case study anytime, any day, for free! All you have to do is observe.

2) Ask others about your communications and conversations – use the Personal Assessment Scorecard located in the back of the book.

Applying this step of the model is very important, because it is critical that you get a sense of what people think about the interactions they have with you. The best way to do this is by describing what you are doing (trying to get feedback on your communications style and skills) and then ask the other party a few key open-ended questions. However, if you are not careful, you will not get the truth from the other party. So, these questions should ideally go to someone you really trust who will give you straight, honest feedback. Some questions you can ask are:

- Do you feel that our conversations are well balanced?
- Do you feel that I have good listening skills?
- Am I easy to talk to?
- How do you think I can improve my communication skills?

In some cases, getting honest feedback can be very difficult, especially if a supervisor is trying to get feedback from subordinates. In this case, I recommend what is called a 360-degree feedback process that allows for anonymous feedback. This will be described in greater detail in the chapter on developing an action plan.

3) Begin to use the process

By this I mean that you think before you talk and try to apply the model. Walk through each step as defined in a conversation with a good friend and then once it is complete, analyze the conversation with your friend.

I recommend that you pick five people initially to do this with – if you are comfortable, tell them what you are doing. A good idea is to pick:

1) A family member
2) A friend
3) A co-worker
4) Your boss or someone in a Position of Authority
5) A clerk in a store or someone who works for you

The above examples most often are very different relationships. And, by choosing a variety of relationships you can see how the balance differs and how you must be consciously adjusting your style and approach to properly match the situation.

4) Practice something I call the 3 Rs:

Rest, Relax and Recharge your voice – Listen!

Try to spend at least 30 minutes with someone and ask as many open ended questions as possible, making sure the balance has more traffic flowing to you than from you. Whatever you do, do not talk more than the other person.

When you choose to talk, do it through clarifying questions for understanding. In this manner, you will essentially learn how to control the traffic pattern. And, then after the conversation, ask the other party how they felt about the balance of the conversation.

You may be surprised that their perception may be that the conversation was very well balanced even if they were talking much more than you were. The tendency of most people is to feel the conversation is well balanced just as long as they are talking 50% or more during the conversation. If that percentage drops below 50%, most people will get a feeling that the conversation was not well balanced. And, you may find that the other party notices a significant improvement in your skills if you normally have the tendency to talk too much.

> The greatest improvement using this model is when the people who talk too much come to realize this, and change their behavior.
>
> The world is full of people who talk more than they should. There is a shortage of people who listen too much.

Listen or thy tongue will keep thee deaf.
American Indian proverb

SUMMARY

How to Apply the Model

Let's recap some easy steps for applying the model. Be sure to use your scorecards as you evaluate your communications.

1) Learn to observe conversations with the Conversation Scorecard -
    a. Spend time watching how people talk to each other with a focus on balance.
    b. Is the conversation balanced when it should be?
    c. How "successful" did the conversation appear to be?
    d. Do you feel that both parties felt good about the outcome?

2) Ask others about you – use the Personal Assessment Scorecard
    a. Start with family members or friends – ask them how they really feel about your communication skills. Do they think it is easy to talk to you or difficult? Seek open, honest feedback and tell them no matter what the response is, you will not get angry – you are trying to learn what people really think.
    b. Discuss the topic with co-workers. Tell them you are trying to improve, and you would like them to describe honestly how they feel about having a conversation with you.
    c. Ask someone you trust as a mentor, pastor, doctor, etc. – basically someone you trust to give you open and honest feedback.
    d. Summarize the findings on your scorecard and look for trends – often single data points are of little value

but trends can be extremely valuable – and remember that perception IS reality.

3) Begin to use the process
    a. Review the process at the end of Chapter 6 and begin to have conversations using these steps. It can help to even tell people what you are doing instead of being nervous about trying to execute something new.
    b. After a phone or face-to-face conversation, write down what you observed. Think of how you could have possibly made that conversation better.
    c. Look for trends in conversations – seek as many conversations as possible that are in balance.

4) Rest, Relax and Recharge your voice – Listen!
    a. Spend 30 minutes with a good friend, perhaps over lunch.
    b. Ask open-ended questions in the conversation.
    c. Make sure you talk less than the other person.
    d. Ask the other party how they felt about the conversation to learn their perception of the balance.

In Chapter 14, we will cover how to develop an Action Plan that can be used to apply the model in a structured way designed specifically for you. You can use the action plan until the process becomes second nature and you can execute it with ease.

Chapter 8

HISTORICAL EXAMPLES OF EXCELLENCE

The Rialto Bridge is the oldest of four bridges to span the Grand Canal in Venice, Italy. It is reported the current Rialto Bridge was designed in the sixteenth century and was born out of a competition to create a stone structure to replace the wooden versions, which had existed here since the 1100s.[6]

Physical bridges can take many different shapes, as is demonstrated when you consider the Rialto Bridge. Communication bridges can be unique also as conversations can be very complex. In the historical examples, we'll look at some unique cases.

---

[6] www.venice-italy-veneto.com, Retrieved 08-02-2011, http://www.venice-italy-veneto.com/the-rialto-bridge-venice-amazing-history-and-facts.html

THE RIALTO BRIDGE

© CAN STOCK PHOTO INC. / EMPRIZE

Examples in History

In discussing historical examples, we will review three different types.

1) Orators
2) Interviewers
3) Conversationalists

ORATORS

In researching examples of good communication skills, often the sources will cite important leaders in history. So, we will review a category of people who excelled in the ability to communicate in the one-to-many situation including famous orators and leaders. Another set of people often cited are those who conduct excellent interviews. In this case, an interview is one person asking another person about a topic or event, sometimes with an audience watching the interview. I call this situation one-to-one-to-many. Finally, there is a group of people who have been consistently cited as great conversationalists. We will look at some of these people and consider this a one-to-one situation.

Clearly, for much of human history, balance has played a key role in many parts of life. And, when it comes to leadership from public figures, there is a term I love to study which is known as "charisma".

Most historical references on this topic center around great communicators such as Winston Churchill, John F. Kennedy, Martin Luther King Jr. and even some people who were very evil like Charles Manson and Adolf Hitler.

Merriam-Webster defines charisma as "a personal magic of leadership arousing special popular loyalty or enthusiasm for a public figure". It also defines charisma as "a special magnetic charm or appeal", where charm is "a trait that fascinates, allures or delights". My theory is that people who have charisma are masters of the ability to balance the bridge. Again, balance does not mean equal flow of information, especially in the context of one-to-many. Instead, balance here is the ability to maintain an appropriate level and balance after understanding what is optimal based on the situation.

Often, those with charisma are described by certain speaking events where it was not only what they said but also how they said it. A key learning here is that more words are not necessarily needed to get your point across and influence your audience or the individual. Timing of the message in the conversation and even a build up to a major point can be very effective.

Winston Churchill was Prime Minister of the United Kingdom twice (1940-45 and 1951-55) and is often referred to as one of the greatest wartime leaders during WWII. He was one of the first leaders during the 1930s to warn about the threat of Nazi Germany. And, when the British people needed inspiration, he would deliver riveting radio broadcasts and speeches. He is widely known for the phrase "We have nothing to fear, but fear itself…" in an attempt to motivate and reassure the British people that ultimately good would triumph over evil in the World War.

In studying Winston Churchill, you learn that although he was not known as a natural orator, he made up for it by hard work and determination. Those around him knew that he would rehearse for long hours on speeches to be delivered to the British people or the House of Commons.

In order to get all of England to understand and adopt his vision, he chose to use simple, but precise language that the entire nation could understand. His communication skills are credited for inspiring people to trust him that Nazi Germany could be defeated. The lesson to learn here is that often communications fail when you fail to be very clear in what you are saying. Using complex terms and vocabulary may sound impressive to some, but often the listener will never get the point unless you can explain things in simple terms.

John F. Kennedy was the 35th President of the United States and is often one of the few presidents that is cited when the topic of charisma is discussed.

He was sworn in as the 35th President at noon on January 20, 1961. In his inaugural address he spoke of the need for all Americans to be active citizens, famously saying, "Ask not what your country can do for you; ask what you can do for your country." He also asked the nations of the world to join together to fight what he called the "common enemies of man: tyranny, poverty, disease, and war itself".

He added: "All this will not be finished in the first one hundred days. Nor will it be finished in the first one thousand days, nor in the life of this Administration, nor even perhaps in our lifetime on this planet. But let us begin." In closing, he expanded on his desire for greater internationalism: "Finally, whether you are citizens of America or citizens of the world, ask of us here the same high standards of strength and sacrifice which we ask of you."

In September and October of 1960, Kennedy appeared with Republican candidate Richard Nixon, then Vice President, in the first televised U.S. presidential debates in U.S. history. During these programs, Nixon, with a sore injured leg and his "five o'clock shadow", looked tense, uncomfortable, and perspiring, while Kennedy, choosing to avail himself of makeup services, appeared relaxed, leading the huge television audience to favor Kennedy as the winner. Radio listeners either thought Nixon had won or that the debates were a draw. The debates are now considered a milestone in American political history—the point at which the medium of television began to play a dominant role in politics.

One of my favorite orators to study is Rev. Dr. Martin Luther King, Jr. Among those who have studied Dr. King and

> The lesson to learn here is that communication effectiveness is not only dependent on the words that you say but how you say them and your appearance, attitude and overall behavior.

what made him a great speaker is Scott Eblin, an executive coach and leadership strategist. Scott points out six qualities that made Dr. King a great speaker. Those six qualities are cadence, context, authenticity, practice, repetition and connection. I agree with these qualities, and when it comes to the bridge analogy, Dr. King was a master in making the "one-to-many bridge" work very well.

Let's look more closely at these six qualities and how they relate to a balanced bridge.

Cadence in this sense almost always meant that King "started out in a slow, measured conversational pace and, over time, increased his pace and his volume as he drew the audience in". [7] As I have listened to the most famous speeches by Dr. King including "I Have a Dream" at the National Mall and "I've Been to the Mountaintop" delivered on the night before he died, you can clearly hear his balanced delivery as if he is a finely tuned aircraft going down the runway for take off. The cadence starts slowly and gradually builds in intensity and volume until the entire audience is airborne, in flight, with him.

The context quality made sure that during his speech he demonstrated how his message and the movement he stood for was an important part of history. Essentially, when he established the bridge, he made it clear to the audience the importance of the connection and why the bridge between them and Dr. King should remain firmly anchored.

The authenticity quality means that King had an overarching story to tell and that his life embodies that story. There was never a

---

[7] www.govexec.com, Retrieved 02-1802013
http://www.govexec.com/excellence/executive-coach/2010/01/
six-qualities-that-made-martin-luther-king-jr-a-great-speaker/39565/

doubt that not only was Dr. King "talking the talk" but he was also "walking the walk" with them.

The practice quality means that Dr. King always took time to prepare so that he didn't have to use extensive notes. This would allow him to improvise and feed off of the reaction of the audience or congregation. Repetition is a common, effective quality of many successful orators. In Dr. King's case, it meant using a phrase such as "I have a dream" or "I didn't stop there" as in the case of the "I've Been to the Mountaintop" speech to help keep the audience focused on the main theme and make it easy to follow him in the speech. In traffic going across the bridge of communication, repetition can be the comfortable consistent messages that make it easy for traffic to flow, such as stay in your lane and maintain a certain speed.

Finally, the connection quality means understanding the energy of the audience and aligning with it. Dr. King was a master at generating energy then allowing the energy to drive him and his enthusiasm. Essentially it can become a bridge where the energy of the traffic is flowing in the most efficient manner possible.

In terms of his ability to balance the communication bridge, I believe that the first five qualities allowed for an extremely powerful connection quality. Dr. King internalized each speech to the point that he could get the bridge firmly anchored and then manage the traffic to achieve maximum effectiveness.

When it comes to people classified as "evil" leaders in history, Adolf Hitler is always near the top of the list. As a general rule, when you study Hitler, you often see short clips of him speaking and most of these clips show what appears to be a raving and ranting madman. However, upon further investigation of his life and his speeches, you find that he actually was a gifted orator who was a master at audience manipulation.

Many sources indicate that Hitler would deliver beer hall speeches that lasted a few hours, common in that day and age in Germany. He would often start the speech in a calm and friendly manner, presenting precise, logical arguments that had been well rehearsed. As the beer would continue to flow and have an impact on the audience, Hitler would take advantage of this and begin to mesmerize them with his voice. It turns out that Hitler was very interested in and had studied mesmerism. Like Dr. King, he used the crescendo technique for wrapping up his speech that would stir the audience to action and cause them to view him as a natural leader and one who could restore Germany to power.

> The more you know about the skills, the more you can be protective of what you should believe when listening to someone deliver a message.

In this case, the techniques used were so powerful that most of the German people could not see that someone who ultimately they would be ashamed of for decades was drawing them in. Like many of the great orators of history, Hitler not only applied his natural abilities, but he used the qualities of preparation, cadence and total conviction to drive home the message. Hitler was a master at establishing a bridge with his audience and then taking advantage of the energy in the room as it would build. In this case, the lesson to be learned is that sometimes these skills can be used to accomplish evil things.

Another example of an evil person who used strong communication skills, at least with willing followers, is Charles Manson, currently in prison. Like Hitler, Manson was effective with communication based upon a very strong conviction and belief that he must control significant events.

Influenced by the music revolution of the 1960s, especially the Beatles, he believed in what he called Helter Skelter, which was a term he took from the song written by the Beatles. He had convinced himself and others that Helter Skelter was going to be an apocalyptic race war, and that his murders would help spur on this war. It's easy to see what most would call insanity when you watch Manson in interviews, but it's also interesting to see how his own conviction of particular ideas and aggressiveness could persuade others.

In fact, the "Manson Family" is a term used for people that were influenced by him and ultimately took orders from him to commit murder. No one can quite be sure why Charles Manson began to believe these things and direct people to commit horrible crimes, but most theories include the fact that he was seeking revenge on a society that had caused him pain and rejection. And, there is no question that his ability to communicate with conviction led him to have a number of devout followers and ultimately altering the way that people think – in his case, he created a bridge with his followers and convinced them with his rhetoric to behave in a certain manner. I would submit that his ability to anchor the bridge with his followers was very strong.

So, what can we learn from those who are classified in history as either being great orators or having charismatic traits that persuaded others?

Powerful phrases, themes and having an overarching life mission are very appealing. Visual appearance can play a very important role – being relaxed and confident. Finally, actual communication delivery seems to be most effective when a message is not only well rehearsed but proper cadence is used to keep the bridge well anchored. Maintaining a direct connection to the audience is critical in order to keep the bridge traffic energized and free flowing until the end of the message. And, the greatest of orators would use a timed crescendo aligned with the mood of the audience for greatest impact.

INTERVIEWERS

Let's move to the second category of excellence in history – great interviewers. Just like great orators, there are many views on this topic and not many qualitative measures to determine the greatest interviewers in history. However, in the school of public opinion, names consistently mentioned include Edward R. Murrow, Dick Cavett, Larry King, David Frost, Barbara Walters and of course, Oprah Winfrey. When you examine this type of list, it becomes apparent that the invention of television had a major impact as it drove the ability for many more people to see and hear an interview.

Of course, there were some radio interviews before television interviews and before radio, there were interviews that simply took place in front of a live audience or for a newspaper, but television is the medium that really allowed classic interviews to become mainstream. This demonstrates the visual importance of a great interview in terms of how the audience experiences the interview.

One of the most interesting names to me is Edward R. Murrow due to the fact that he began in radio prior to television but then made the transition to television and is widely respected as one of the greatest American journalists in history. His peers admired the honesty and integrity with which he delivered information.

And, at a time when Senator Joe McCarthy was powerful and feared due to his tactics, Murrow produced a series of television shows that helped lead to the censure of the senator. Murrow had the ability to balance the bridge with those he encountered so that the American people could get an honest view of the news of the day – this began with radio reports during WW II in the late 1930s and ended in television by 1960.

It's important to understand the skills of great interviewers. As you learn more about balancing the communication bridge, you can apply these skills as appropriate.

Great interviewers follow all of the steps in Balance the Bridge, but with a main goal of getting the person who is being interviewed to talk openly about a particular topic or issue. In doing this, the audience gets an opportunity to either learn new things about a topic or person or perhaps simply confirm or deny preconceived beliefs. I decided to cover the topic of interviewers in this section so that you can understand these specific skills and then watch for them in observing the interviewers of today.

Most experts that discuss how best to interview someone to get the best results talk about having a conversation rather than just asking questions. This means being flexible enough to "go with the flow" and keep the person comfortable rather than making it feel like an inquisition.

When you do pose a question, it's critical that you ask open-ended questions designed to get the person to open up and elaborate on the topic. In addition, a powerful technique is to stay silent for four or five seconds after the person finishes an answer, which often will cause them to speak a bit more, and these comments may be the most valuable and least rehearsed part of their answer. In our bridge analogy, it is your job as the interviewer to set up the initial bridge and begin the conversation so that you invite the flow of traffic with thought provoking statements and open-ended questions. Above all, you need to have a specific goal for the interview. It could be as simple as having the person describe some particular accomplishments that are of interest or the goal may be much more complicated.

A common trait of the previously named famous interviewers is that just about all of them are considered journalists, reporters or "hosts" of some type of show. It is therefore second nature to them to report on a particular topic or investigate something that will have great interest to the audience.

All of them have the ability to communicate well and also educate the audience at the same time. This certainly begins with preparation and passion but when the bridge is anchored, it then becomes a primary job to manage the flow of traffic in order to serve the needs of the audience and not simply the needs of the two people having the conversation. The needs of the audience drive the interviewer and thus the interviewer must keep the interview on track.

In the famous Frost/Nixon interviews in 1977, Sir David Frost initially had a very tough time controlling the interview and the flow of traffic across the bridge. Nixon had resigned in 1974 and had spent a few years out of the public life after the Presidential pardon by Gerald Ford. Nixon believed that he could easily control Frost, and in fact, for a number of days did just that. However, Frost in the end of taping, due to his unrelenting preparation and persistence, finally was able to get Nixon to speak directly about the obstruction of justice charge, and Nixon famously confessed that he had "let the American people down", and essentially admitted that he had participated in the obstruction of justice. Nixon stated at this point in the interview "… When the President does it, that means it's not illegal…".

When watching the interview skills of today's best including Barbara Walters and Oprah Winfrey, pay particular attention to how they balance the bridge during an interview. And, look for their open-ended questions that essentially open the bridge for traffic to flow to them.

CONVERSATIONALISTS

Our last category in history we will examine is the Conversationalist. Jon Spayed, co-author of the book Salons: The Joy of Conversation, published his list over 10 years ago of the greatest conversationalists of all time. This list includes Socrates, Martin Luther, Catherine De Rambouillet and Carl Rogers to name a few. In this article, Jon writes "…*Great conversationalists are often, but not always, great talkers. The men and women honored here stand out for the way they fostered great conversation—as brilliant speakers, as powerful listeners, or as figures who masterfully facilitated the exchange of ideas. Drawing upon the wisdom, skill, and joie de vivre they brought to the simple act of talking, we can all learn a thing or two about the art of conversation….*".[8]

When you study Socrates, the Greek Philosopher who lived from 469 – 399 B.C., it is easy to see how he stimulated conversation and dialogue. History often credits him as one of the founders of

---

[8] www.utne.com, Retrieved 02-20-2013
http://www.utne.com/2002-07-01/the-greatest-conversationalists-of-all-time.aspx

Western Philosophy, and certainly his conversational skills helped him to lead his followers and students. In addition to influencing others with his own thoughts and opinions he knew how to skillfully facilitate discussion.

When more than 2 people get together for a conversation, it's almost always a good idea to have a facilitator. This doesn't always have to be a formal role, but the skilled communicator can play this role using Balance the Bridge techniques. In the work environment that will be discussed later, I recommend that for all meetings there is clarity up front on who is facilitating, who is taking notes and who is keeping time. Meetings become much more effective and enjoyable when there is order rather than meeting chaos which we all have witnessed, even in many top companies around the globe.

Martin Luther, who lived from 1483 – 1546, is credited for initiating the Protestant Reformation by the posting of his 95 Theses as a way of declaring disagreement with many practices within the Roman Catholic Church at that time. While many of his ideas were controversial, he was able to stimulate thought provoking discussions that have influenced Christianity for centuries.

Martin Luther was very skilled at not only preaching his ideas, but also attracted many people with his conversation style around the dinner table. He was able to show empathy for people and essentially teach them at the same time. By creating this type of balance, the impact on people was far greater than if he had not practiced balanced communication skills.

By the time of the 17th and 18th century, a phenomenon had developed in Europe that was very important in the history of women's rights – it was called a "salon". At that time, in a male dominated world, a number of very intelligent, skilled women formed an environment that was essentially a forum for conversation.

The salons had major influence on important people of the time, both men and women. In that setting, women were able to freely express their opinions and thus they could have an impact on everything from politics to religion. Catherine De Rambouillet (1588 – 1665) started the first important salon in Paris at the Hotel Pisani, which later became known as the Hotel de Rambouillet. One interesting characteristic of this salon and most others was the fact that good manners were practiced and taught.

Balance the Bridge certainly emphasizes the use of good manners in the 5 steps, and good manners appear to be something that is being lost as we've moved into the 21st century. You will find that developing and using good manners is a key competitive differentiator. The salon started by Catherine continued for 50 years and had a major influence on many people in France and throughout Europe. There was plenty of variety of discussion and entertainment including comedies and concerts - not just serious discussion. It is my belief that the practice of good manners and excellent communication skills in the salons helped to form the foundation for women to be considered equal to men in all aspects of ideas and thinking. These skilled salon hosts were masters at balancing the bridge.

There are many more examples that we could visit in history – but the last person I will discuss is Carl Rogers (1902 – 1987) who was an influential American psychologist. He is widely known to be among the founders of what is called the client-centered approach to psychology, which focuses on the client's capacity for self-direction. Essentially, he believed that each human has one basic motive – that is to self-actualize or to reach one's full potential.

> *The most interesting part of the client-centered approach is something called reflective listening.*

Reflective listening, the most interesting part of the client-centered approach, essentially involves first listening closely to understand the idea (or traffic coming across the bridge to you) and then stating the idea back to the other party to confirm that you understand the idea correctly. This is an extremely powerful technique to use in balancing the bridge.

First of all, if you have not understood the idea correctly, you will immediately find out. I like to coach people to use this technique especially during conversations with their boss. All too often people make mistakes at work because they basically perform a task with a thought in mind that actually is not what the boss wanted them to do. And, people in general like to hear their own ideas played back to them – it helps to assure them that you were actually listening to what they had to say.

Reflective listening is a very easy and effective technique for those who have not yet established excellent communication skills. Essentially, it is a "safety-net" that you can use right away to begin to make sure that you have heard correctly what the other person is trying to communicate to you.

Now, let's move on to some current examples of excellence.

Chapter 9

EXAMPLES OF
EXCELLENCE – TODAY

It took almost 4 years to build the Hangzhou Bay Bridge across the bay southwest of Shanghai, China. However, the cable-stayed bridge took nearly a decade to design and almost 600 experts participated in the design phase due to the challenging conditions that exist with the construction of such a long bridge and the extreme weather in this part of the world. In the end, the 22-mile bridge reduced the travel time by 1.5 hours between Ningbo and Shanghai. It opened in 2007 as one of the longest bridges over water in the world. It has 6 lanes in both directions and has a service center in the middle of the bridge that includes a hotel, gas station, restaurant and rest area. Now that's a modern bridge!

As you build communication bridges you will find that some are more complex than others to build, but with determination the bridge can become very powerful and serve you well.

THE HANGZHOU BAY BRIDGE

TALENTED TALK SHOW HOSTS

Living in the Atlanta area, we have an abundance of sunshine, traffic and great talk show hosts. I make it a habit to listen to one of our radio stations often, WSB, which is a News/Talk station because the variety of talk show hosts and their different styles. It makes for a virtual sea of examples on this topic. The subject of the show and the entertainment factor is a good reason to listen, but I also listen to observe the talent that different people have in Balancing the Bridge. Plus, this is a very sophisticated example where they not only must create and balance the bridge with whoever calls in to the show but they also have an audience of millions who are observing the conversation.

Essentially the audience is a participant in the conversation who never gets to talk. However, the audience knows that their role is only to listen and thus this is an accepted expectation by the audience. They may become motivated to dial in to talk on a subject (I have done so on more than one occasion), but this is a very small fraction of listeners. If the conversations are of interest, the audience will continue listening to the show and the talk show host will survive and often thrive in syndication.

This works well due to the fact that listeners enjoy hearing the conversations, especially if the caller is expressing the listener's opinion or an opinion that is completely opposite. Also, many listeners are simply trying to learn from the information presented in the conversation.

Personalities such as Clark Howard, Neal Boortz, Herman Cain and Wes Moss, just to name a few, all have very different styles and agendas.

Clark Howard is a consumer advocate guru who can help you "save more, spend less and avoid getting ripped off" to quote the slogan that always begins the show. In addition to the subject being of interest to a very large audience, Clark has what seems to be an infinite set of knowledge about all sorts of consumer topics. This, however, is not enough. The magic comes into play with his style, delivery and the way he establishes the bridge between he and the caller. Once the bridge is established, he is a master at balance.

A great example of establishing the bridge is in the opening question. He often will say something like "Bob now joins us on the Clark Howard show... Bob, how are you and **how can I be of service to you?**" On the surface, this may seem trivial, but let's examine this more closely. "How are you" is a great way to open a conversation as it demonstrates to the other person that you have an interest in them. Then, by asking "How can I be of service?" he immediately opens the door for the caller to speak of his or her problem with an implication that he will "serve" them.

Even though Clark is in control and essentially has the Position of Authority, he knows that he must put the caller at ease and give them the opportunity to speak about their problem or ask their question.

And, he comes across as genuine, because he is genuine. I have witnessed Clark Howard doing many things to help people such as Habitat for Humanity sponsorship, Clark's Kids at Christmas time and the list goes on and on. The magic of the dialogue occurs not only due to his knowledge, but also in his ability to establish the bridge and manage the traffic. Open-ended questions coupled with good advice and time management keeps the callers calling and the listeners listening.

Neal Boortz is another example of a skilled communicator, but with a much different style of delivery and bridge management. The premise of his show

> *Your core personality and approach can influence all conversations.*

is "Somebody has got to say it"… implying that the topics to be discussed are the raw, hard truth that people often ignore or are unwilling to face since it may not be pleasant. He constantly harps on the fact that most Americans are ignorant of our laws, government, and the constitution and frankly are not willing to accept personal responsibility.

Neal's popularity is similar to the popularity of other conservative talk show hosts such as Sean Hannity and Rush Limbaugh, but he has a unique style that I find fascinating which is the ability to manage any type of caller. He is known as the "Talkmaster" and is clear about his Position of Authority – you can earn the right to have a dialogue with him if in the first 10-15 seconds or so you can demonstrate a logical point on a particular subject. If you ramble, state an opinion as if it were fact without evidence or demonstrate ignorance on a particular topic you then become easy prey for the master and entertainment for millions of listeners as Neal proceeds to bury you in the conversation.

So, this bridge is only meant to be balanced if you can speak with facts to back up your opinions – one slip up and he flips the switch to a situation where you no longer are given the gift of a balanced bridge with him. This simple equation worked every day until his retirement a few years ago with millions of listeners that loved to witness it.

With Neal Boortz retiring after 42 years of hosting talk radio shows, Herman Cain took over his show. Herman has many of the same conservative values as Neal, but his personality and delivery is at times much different. Early in the 2012 Presidential Election primaries, he was a serious contender as a Republican candidate.

In addition to having some very good ideas on how to run the nation and offering solutions to many problems, Herman is well liked because of his communication skills and his ability to balance the bridge with anyone. He does very well with people from all walks of life, and even when a caller disagrees with him, he shows patience and good manners which is something that you rarely see in television or radio personalities anymore. He uses a powerful theme, often stated as "they THINK we are stupid", implying that our current government officials believe they are much smarter than the hard working, voting public and Herman is out to prove this wrong.

Herman is a great example of someone who used strong communication skills and determination throughout his life to advance his career. In his professional life, he ultimately was promoted to CEO of Godfather's Pizza and the National Restaurant Organization before getting involved in national politics and launching a successful career as a radio talk show host.

Wes Moss is the host of Money Matters, a show about investing and preparing for retirement. Wes typically begins his show with a monologue on what has happened over the past week in the financial world. Then, he bridges the facts of the week to the callers by emphasizing that no matter what happens during the week, the strategy of income investing is sound and that he is there to help all listeners understand how to employ the strategy.

Wes stresses that income investing to fill the gap that is needed, when considering the retirement income the listener will need, is the best strategy. He then consistently explains that income investing is all about portfolio yield, which comes from dividends, interest and distributions. Finally, inviting the callers to explain their questions and

> *Having a consistent message in times of uncertainty can be very powerful when you are communicating to a large audience.*

concerns and then providing simple answers is what keeps people listening to Wes.

It's all about the ability to balance a consistent message and allowing each caller to express his or her unique needs and concerns.

PRESIDENT BARACK OBAMA

At the time of this writing, Barack Obama is in his second term as President of the United States. Whether or not you agree with his policies or position on topics of interest, it is easy to see examples of his excellent ability to communicate.

Over the years, he has developed the skills that allow him to captivate the masses in the U.S. when he delivers a speech. His communication skills helped to get him re-elected even though statistics show that the quantitative results of his first term were less than stellar. In all of U.S. history, there are many examples of Presidents failing to get re-elected when specific quantitative measures such as unemployment percentage were at the current levels.

This is a lesson for everyone to learn on the power of communication and perception. In an article on Obama's 2008 victory speech, Olivia Mitchell wrote on Six Lessons in Public Speaking from Obama.[9]

The six lessons include:

1) Know your audience,
2) Envelop your point in a story,
3) Paint pictures on the canvas of your audience's mind,
4) Get personal,
5) Wait for the weight and
6) Light and shade.

Lessons 1-4 are fairly straight forward, but lessons 5 and 6 require more focus and skill. "Wait for the weight" talks to the fact that Obama is not in a hurry. He waits for the audience to process and react to his statements or proposals. In doing this, he gives his words more "weight". This is another example of balancing the bridge between the speaker and the audience. In this case, the speaker is controlling the traffic and the speed of the traffic.

"Light and Shade" speaks to different moods such as joyful, humorous, serious, determined, etc. The contrasts of moods keep the audience engaged according to Mitchell. In balance the bridge, this refers to the **type** of traffic going across the bridge, and is a very important concept. We've all talked with someone who has no contrast in how they are speaking, which often causes the other party to lose interest or be far less engaged in the conversation, making it harder to maintain a good anchor on the bridge.

---

[9] www.speakingaboutpresenting.com, Retrieved 02-26-13
http://www.speakingaboutpresenting.com/content/lessons-public-speaking-obama/

The lesson to learn here is that the variance of moods in a presentation or conversation can really help to keep the bridge anchor in place.

PRESIDENT BILL CLINTON

Finally we look at Bill Clinton, the 42nd US President who was in office from 1993 to 2001. According to a CNN report, citing the required annual financial disclosure report of Secretary of State Hillary Clinton, Bill Clinton earned $13.4M in speaking fees in 2011. Since he left the White House in 2001, he has earned $89M for speeches (through July 2012).[10]

What makes Clinton such a sought after speaker? Well, for starters, he's really good at it. Whether or not you agree with his political views or his performance as President, the numbers speak for themselves on his ability to generate income from groups willing to pay large sums of money for a guest speaker.

Clinton is a great example of someone today who is a successful speaker, and has learned to follow the techniques that have generated some of the greatest speeches in history. Essentially, he has become a master of balancing the bridge, one-to-many, by forming a solid anchor with the audience, then managing the traffic and the energy in the room.

In addition, his speech to nominate Barack Obama for a second term as President was widely judged to be an excellent speech (even if you don't agree with the content). Why? In Rebecca Boyle's

---

[10] www.cnn.com, Retrieved 02-26-13
http://www.cnn.com/2012/07/03/politics/clinton-speaking-fees

article in Popular Science after Clinton's speech at the Democratic National Convention, she explains that Clinton is the master at delivering a speech that starts with a preconceived idea then is supported by evidence supporting that idea.[11] She goes on to cite Greta Stahl and Nancy Duarte who are experts in communication who claim that Clinton is a master at the basics including:

1) Understand your audience and target your words appropriately
2) Build the speech around a big idea
3) Balance emotion and fact (there's that balance word again!)
4) Make it your own
5) Exploit contrasts

Nancy Duarte has gone so far as to chart the mechanics of great speeches and has developed a model that many great speeches follow. Her model includes the speaker talking about the negative "what is" and the positive "what could be". In many famous speeches, the speaker will go back and forth between what is and what could be, gradually building emotion to the point that in the end what could be becomes something she calls the "new bliss". Essentially, this is ending on a high note that has the audience in frenzy, as in Martin Luther King, Jr.'s speech generally known as "I have a dream". And, although Clinton has a habit of long speeches, we know by history that speeches don't have to be long to be effective. Martin Luther King delivered his "I have a dream" speech in 16 minutes.

Let's now move on to some case studies that will help you clearly understand how to use Balance the Bridge.

---

[11] www.popsci.com, Retrieved 02-26-13
http://www.popsci.com/science/article/2012-09/
fyi-why-bill-clinton-so-good-speaking-crowd

Chapter 10

CASE STUDIES

The Chapel Bridge in Lucerne, Switzerland is unique in that it is perhaps the oldest wooden, covered footbridge in the world. It was built in 1333 A.D. and spans across the Reuss River. A large portion of the bridge was unfortunately destroyed by fire in 1993, but the bridge was rebuilt in 1994. It is still the oldest surviving truss bridge in the world, over 500 feet in length. As you cross the bridge, you are treated to paintings on interior triangular frames, some dating back to the 17th century.

Your communication bridges may appear simple at first, but upon deeper examination may be complex and well illustrated! Pay close attention to the bridge for hidden treasures.

THE CHAPEL BRIDGE

© CAN STOCK PHOTO INC. / OLGYSHA

Reviewing Case Studies can help you to understand the model in greater detail by looking at real life situations. Let's begin by looking again at the six fundamental types of relationships and situations:

Relationship	Situation	Example
Peer-to-Peer	One-to-One	Two friends talking
Peer-to-Peer	One-to-Few	Four friends having lunch
Peer-to-Peer	One-to-Many	Committee member presenting to large committee of equals
Position of Authority	One-to-One	Boss and employee
Position of Authority	One-to-Few	Drill Sergeant with three Privates
Position of Authority	One-to-Many	CEO of a company addressing 300 employees

The structure of each Case Study will include:

1) Background Information
2) A Conversation or Event
3) A Scorecard from the Conversation or Event
4) Conclusion and Recommendations

The Scorecard will have six questions and an overall score. The overall score will result in one of three conclusions:

1) **Not Successful** – The conversation or event had an unsuccessful outcome and one or more of the steps of the process need improvement.
2) **Moderately Successful** – The conversation or event had a successful outcome, but one or more of the steps of the process need improvement.
3) **Successful** – The conversation or event had a successful outcome and all steps of the process are on track.

CASE STUDY #1: PEER-TO-PEER, ONE-TO-ONE

Sue was in the grocery store when she noticed that Alice was coming down her aisle. They've been friends for years, playing on the same subdivision tennis team and going to the same church.

However, Sue knows that a conversation with Alice will never be short, as Alice loves to talk. Recently Alice's husband Bob was laid off by his company, and Alice has decided to go back to work. Alice has a degree in marketing and worked for many years at a high tech company shortly after she and Bob got married. Sue currently works for a small software company that has been doing very well for the past 10 years, and is now starting to challenge the big players in the healthcare software market.

Sue's company is growing and they have openings in the Marketing department, and Sue knows the VP of Marketing very well. Although Sue is in a hurry, she knows she needs to talk to Alice as they approach each other.

The conversation begins in the grocery aisle, and as usual after a brief "Hello, how are you?" from each of them, Alice launches into a long story to give Sue an update on what has been going on since they last talked. They are forced to move their grocery carts many times due to the fact that other people are trying to shop and get to items on the shelves.

As the conversation continues, Alice does 90% of the talking even though Sue tries to do more than just listen. At the 10 minute mark, Alice is going on and on about how she really needs to get a job and has been looking now for 3 months with no luck.

Sue encourages her to keep looking, and relates that with her experience she certainly should find something soon. Alice asks if there are any openings at Sue's company for someone like her, and Sue promises to check on this. Feeling a bit uncomfortable, Sue begins to grab her cart and closes the conversation by saying that she has an appointment, but that it was good to see Alice and wishes her luck in the job search.

Alice moves on down the aisle thinking of what a great conversation they just had – she is sure that Sue will call her and provide introductions in her company so that Alice can be considered. Sue moves on to the next aisle thinking "Same ole Alice – just doesn't know when to stop talking…too bad because if she had better communication skills I would recommend her, but there's no way I will chance my reputation by introducing her. She would talk everyone to death."

The result of this conversation included a completely different feeling by the two people talking. Unfortunately, Alice, who has poor communication skills, and is oblivious to this fact, believes that it was a good conversation. Sue, who does have good communication skills once again experienced that Alice does 90% of the talking in any conversation they have, and has very poor listening skills. Although Sue's company has openings for someone with Alice's experience, Sue is reluctant to bring this up with Alice as she is worried about her own reputation if she would recommend someone who has such poor listening skills.

Conversation Scorecard - Alice	Y/N	Supporting Evidence
Was the Relationship recognized?	Y	This one was easy for Alice – she is a peer of Sue's – no problem here.
Was the Situation recognized?	Y	The situation was one-to-one – again, no problem.
Was the Bridge Anchored?	N	Alice never attempts to anchor the bridge – she immediately started talking.
Was the Traffic Managed?	N	This was the big problem – Alice did 90% of the talking.
Was the Bridge closed appropriately?	N	Sue rushed off just to get away – no effective close here.
Was there a Successful Outcome?	N	No chance for Alice to get recommended due to the above problems.
Overall Score	2/6	**Not Successful** - This conversation did not have a successful outcome and many steps of the process need improvement.

The key learning of this Case Study is that since Alice did not balance the bridge, she missed out on a potential job opportunity, and won't understand why Sue never introduces her to the potential hiring manager.

CASE STUDY #2: PEER-TO-PEER, ONE-TO-FEW

One of my favorite movies from a few years ago is "Julie and Julia". It's basically a story about a young writer named Julie who decides to write a blog for 365 days on Julia Child, basically cooking all 524 recipes in her cookbook over that period of time.

In this movie, Julie has lunch with 3 of her very successful friends who are all pre-occupied with their own successful life. It's a classic example of poor communication skills and very funny to watch. If you get a chance to watch it, you'll see many things to avoid in a peer-to-peer, one-to-few lunch and conversation.

The night before, Julie describes the lunch the next day to be the "ritual cobb salad lunch" and how she is dreading it. The lunch begins with Julie meeting the other 3 at a nice restaurant. They each order a cobb salad but each cobb salad is slightly different.

Even as the scene began, one friend was already talking on a cell phone. She hangs up and complains about her assistant, and another friend joins in complaining about her assistant. It becomes obvious that the other 3 are living a very different life than Julie. A cell phone rings next and the friend immediately picks up the call, demonstrating that the phone call is more important than the conversation with friends. She is making a real estate deal, and after she hangs up, the other 2 friends toast the deal. Julie reluctantly joins the toast.

At that point, one of the friends says "And enough about you, here's to me!" and begins to brag about a recent job promotion. Then, one of the friends asks "So, how's your job, Julie?" (Julie is currently working at a crisis management hot line organization where 9/11 victims can call in if they are seriously depressed or suicidal, and those like Julie who answer the phone try to help or point them to government resources they can use to help their situation.) Julie tries to answer, but 2 of the friends don't even allow her to speak. Instead, they immediately interrupt her and make their own comments on how bad and how sad it must be.

Right about that time, 2 more cell phones ring that are answered and the third friend begins talking into her voice recorder, leaving Julie alone at the table, frustrated. The scene ends with the friend using the voice recorder asking Julie if she could interview Julie for an article she is writing. Julie agrees but the friend then immediately looks at her calendar and says "I am so busy, I just don't know when I can fit you in". Julie, again frustrated, says "May I remind you that you are the one who wants to see me?"

The scene in this movie is less than 3 minutes long, but there are a plethora of examples to learn from here. For the person watching the movie, you immediately can tell that although these ladies are perhaps very good friends of Julie, they each have serious communication problems, and are oblivious to this fact.

Making matters worse, the other 3 appear to be very successful, so they have little to no incentive to change. However, their lack of success in communication skills will certainly limit their potential.

Technology such as cell phones will be discussed in greater detail later in the book. As the scene begins the use of cell phones at a lunch is the first example of how the other friends are perfectly willing to put their lunch conversations "on hold" if a call comes in, essentially telling the friends who are face-to-face that the caller is more important.

Certainly, there are times when a cell phone call would be more important, but the best practice here is to always apologize for having to take a call. And, keeping the call very brief plus apologizing again after you hang up is critical to make sure the person you are face to face with understands the logic behind the priority of the call. Many good communicators will actually warn the face-to-face friend that their cell phone is on and they may have to take a particular call (sick family member, urgent work situation, etc.)

The next great example is when one friend says "Enough about you, here's to me!" and begins to brag. Although this is an extreme case as the friend actually made the statement, I constantly witness people making this mistake without actually saying those words. Instead, they simply try to dominate the conversation with something they are proud of – their kids, their house, their job, and the list goes on and on. We then witness 3 more mistakes. When asked about her job, 2 of the friends interrupt Julie and don't allow her to answer. Then, we find 2 of the friends answering cell calls and the third friend talking into her voice recorder so Julie is left to sit at the table essentially alone.

The final mistake is her friend asking if Julie would be willing to be interviewed, but then turning the table and telling Julie she has no time on the calendar.

The result of the lunch in the 3-minute scene is that Julie feels completely frustrated by all of the conversations. There was no attempt by any of the 3 friends to establish a bridge with Julie and/or manage the traffic to allow Julie some time to actually speak. The 3 friends who each had poor communication skills, were very comfortable interrupting each other. They had obviously gotten very used to communicating in this manner, and had no clue that Julie felt left out.

Although this movie scene is funny, we can learn much from it on how to avoid the mistakes that can happen in peer-to-peer, one-to-few conversations.

Let's look at a Conversation Scorecard which is a bit more complex, but we'll "grade" the 3 friends:

Conversation Scorecard - Friends	Y/N	Supporting Evidence
Was the Relationship recognized?	Y	The four friends are peer-to-peer. No real problem here.
Was the Situation recognized?	N	This was a one-to-few but there was no attempt to establish multiple bridges.
Was the Bridge Anchored?	N	Although Julie offered an anchor on her side, none of the three accepted the offer to anchor a bridge more than a few seconds.
Was the Traffic Managed?	N	Not a chance – lots of interruptions and talking over each other.
Was the Bridge closed appropriately?	N	There was no attempt at closing any bridge, largely because they never were established in the first place.
Was there a Successful Outcome?	N	Julie left the lunch even more frustrated than before, and she had low expectations to begin with.
Overall Score	1/6	**Not Successful** – This event did not have a successful outcome and almost all of the steps of the process need improvement.

CASE STUDY #3: – PEER-TO-PEER, ONE-TO-MANY

George lives in a swim/tennis subdivision and he is on the board of the homeowner's association. The subdivision has no sidewalks, but other subdivisions in the area that were built more recently have sidewalks. This has caused a number of homeowners to speak out to consider the installation of sidewalks as an upgrade to the subdivision. George happens to be one of the homeowners who likes the idea of new sidewalks, as his wife Sara and their 3 young kids frequently walk their dog and ride bikes in the subdivision.

The homeowner's association has planned a meeting to allow all homeowners to hear a proposal the board believes would make sense. George has agreed to do the presentation as he collected almost all the information from the company that the board selected as the best possible vendor. The vendor offered to come do the proposal, but the board decided that it would be best if the presentation was done by one of the board members.

George has been a successful CPA for a number of years and his customers really like him. His communication skills are very good one-on-one, but he rarely stands up in front of a group to talk, and when he does he frequently gets nervous. Nevertheless, he is passionate on this topic and he prepares his presentation, complete with slides and example photos.

On the night of the presentation, almost 100 people attend the meeting, causing the board to have to get some additional chairs at the last minute. Never has there been a subdivision meeting this well attended.

It becomes obvious in pre-meeting conversations that this is a very controversial topic, with strong feelings on both sides. On one side, many families with small children are very positive about the project, even though each family in the subdivision might be assessed $400-$500 to cover the cost. On the other side, there are many who are skeptical that the sidewalks put in after the fact would not look right, and the possible assessment is a roadblock.

George begins the presentation by jumping into the slides without setting any ground rules. It becomes obvious that George wants this project to move forward, and his style and intensity show this with each slide that gets presented. When a neighbor who is supportive of the project asks a question, George is happy to give much information to answer the question. However, when a neighbor who is known to be against the project asks a question, George delivers a very quick response, in some ways demonstrating that the question was not even pertinent.

George plans to cover everything in an hour, but he has 75 slides and many are hard to read, especially from the back of the room. Although he is pushing hard to get through the material, an hour goes by, and George is only on slide 33. The audience is getting frustrated due to the fact that many people are interrupting George with questions. Some people are calling out "let him finish!" and others feel that he is not an unbiased presenter. As the talking in the crowd becomes more frequent, it becomes obvious to the President of the homeowner's association that they will not be able to finish the presentation and take a vote. The President stands up and thanks George for presenting the material he was able to get through, and tells the group that another meeting will be scheduled to continue the discussion.

The results of this meeting were nowhere close to the goals of George and the board. Instead of an opportunity for civil discussion leading to a vote and a decision, there was frustration and confusion.

What were the causes and issues? The board failed to realize that with such a controversial topic, a facilitator who was neutral should have led the presentation, or George should have presented as a neutral party even though he had an opinion. George failed to balance the bridge with the neighbors who were against the proposal. He managed the traffic differently depending on who was asking a question. He set no ground rules up front and he was unrealistic on the amount of material that could be covered in one hour.

Balancing the bridge in a one-to-many situation, especially when it is peer-to-peer, means checking for understanding regularly and having realistic goals on what can be accomplished in the presentation.

Many excellent presenters practice a few rules that are easy to remember. One rule is the "Rule of 3". This is a popular method that has been used by great speakers from Thomas Jefferson to Ronald Regan to Steve Jobs. The concept here is to break things down to 3 specific things. Many experts on public speaking believe that people can more easily understand and remember things if they come in 3s. Just as when Thomas Jefferson wrote in the Declaration of Independence the phrase "...life, liberty and the pursuit of happiness..." or when Steve Jobs introduced the iPad 2 in 2011 as "... thinner, lighter and faster than the original...", you can also use the rule of 3 in presentations.

George was trying to send too much traffic across the bridge to the group of 100 in too short a period of time. Traffic eventually jammed and over half of the traffic never made it.

This is a relatively complex case study, but let's apply the Conversation Scorecard to George:

Conversation Scorecard -George	Y/N	Supporting Evidence
Was the Relationship recognized?	N	George did not recognize this was peer-to-peer. His attitude was that he was in a Position-of-Authority.
Was the Situation recognized?	N	Although George knew he was presenting to a large group, he did not use effective skills in managing the one-to-many situation.
Was the Bridge Anchored?	N	George made no attempts to anchor the bridge – instead his agenda was to get through the material.
Was the Traffic Managed?	N	Because he was trying to cover too much information, and because his opinion was strong, he was talking unless he was interrupted. Too much info to cover in the time allowed did not allow for balanced traffic flow.
Was the Bridge closed appropriately?	N	The President of the HOA had to step in to end the discussion – enough said.
Was there a Successful Outcome?	N	In addition to failing to meet the desired outcome of the presentation, this presentation probably ruined the chances for future presentations on the topic.
Overall Score	0/6	**Not Successful** – This event did not have a successful outcome, and all of the steps of the process need improvement.

CASE STUDY #4: POSITION-OF-AUTHORITY, ONE-TO-ONE

Mark has been working for Alicia for 6 months. He is a marketing specialist and handles all of the events that the sales force participates in such as trade shows. It's his job to make sure that the events are a success and that the sales force gains the maximum number of leads from each event.

Alicia's marketing team consists of 8 specialists, many who are generating collateral for sales and creating competitive presentations. Since Mark lives in Charlotte with Alicia in Atlanta, they talk over the phone, but rarely get a chance to see each other face-to-face due to company travel restrictions. Mark needed to be in Atlanta to attend a customer meeting, so they took the opportunity to have a 6-month review of Mark's work, face-to-face.

Before the meeting, Mark prepared a list of the 3 most important things to cover with Alicia. The list included:

1) Accomplishments over the last 6 months,
2) Current top priorities, and
3) Plan for the next 90 days.

When the meeting began, Mark thanked Alicia for being willing to meet him and allowed her to set the tone for the discussion while he listened carefully. He then asked a few clarifying questions and repeated back the answers on occasion to make sure he understood in a way that made Alicia feel that he was following her very well.

When Alicia signaled that they should move to Mark's prepared list, he began to go through it, periodically emphasizing that each item was based upon what he thought he heard from her as direction the last time they met. Alicia was impressed that Mark was very well organized in his informal review, and although she made a few minor corrections on priority, she was impressed with the 90-day plan that she had not asked for. She mentioned to Mark that it was a great idea, and that she would probably have the other 7 staff members complete a 90 day plan for her, using this as a best practice.

Throughout the entire meeting, Mark tried to make good eye contact and used good reflective listening skills when Alicia would talk. So that he would not do all the talking, he asked some open-ended questions periodically to make sure there was a good balance of traffic flowing across the well-established bridge. As Mark has only worked for Alicia for 6 months, he was careful to make sure that she was always in Position of Authority. His role of subordinate needed to be respectful of her position, but also allow him to demonstrate his results and the plan going forward in order to make sure he was on the right track.

He summarized what he learned from Alicia at the end of the meeting and clarified with her his understanding of the feedback and direction he received.

The meeting lasted an hour and Mark headed for the airport. After Mark left, Alicia felt as though she had made a great decision to hire him. Not only was he off to a good start, but also in a year or two, he could be a good candidate to replace her if she got promoted.

The result of this conversation was a very effective meeting. Mark's preparation and communication skills immediately made a good impression on his new boss.

Mark's ability to recognize the relationship and situation, plus his ability to visualize and establish the bridge, manage the traffic and close the bridge appropriately made the conversation very comfortable for both of them.

Conversation Scorecard - Mark	Y/N	Supporting Evidence
Was the Relationship recognized?	Y	Mark recognized Alicia's position of authority throughout the meeting.
Was the Situation recognized?	Y	This was a one-to-one situation, and easy for Mark to recognize.
Was the Bridge Anchored?	Y	Mark used techniques up front to firmly anchor the bridge.
Was the Traffic Managed?	Y	Mark not only had prepared a concise list to cover, but also used reflective listening skills and open-ended questions to make sure traffic was balanced.
Was the Bridge closed appropriately?	Y	Mark specifically used techniques to close the bridge on this conversation including summarizing what he heard from her in the meeting.
Was there a Successful Outcome?	Y	Alicia was pleased with his progress and he left knowing that he was on the right track. Mission accomplished.
Overall Score	6/6	**Successful** – This conversation had a successful outcome and all of the steps of the process were on track!

CASE STUDY #5: POSITION-OF-AUTHORITY, ONE-TO-FEW

Tom is a supply chain section manager and his department and has a staff of 6 people. There's quite a bit of talent across his team – 4 of the six have over 15 years of experience and 2 of the team members are new hires who are young and full of great new ideas. The 4 experienced people are Bob, Chandler, Shirley and Mary. Brent and Larisa are the new hires, just out of college.

The mission of Tom's organization is to maximize the efficiency of the suppliers to the company. There are buyers that negotiate pricing and issue purchase orders, but Tom's group interfaces with R&D and Sales to make sure that the right suppliers are in place and they constantly are evaluating new possible suppliers that may be able to produce higher quality products for a better price.

Recently, the company has seen profits decline, and there are many cost cutting efforts going on to reverse this trend. Tom's boss has asked him to bring new ideas and solutions that will further optimize the supply chain. Tom is under pressure and calls a team meeting to brainstorm the ideas.

The meeting begins at 9am and everyone is there but Bob. He is notoriously late for meetings, but both R&D and Sales love him, and Tom is reluctant to criticize his tardiness. Tom knows that Bob has received offers from other organizations and if he loses Bob now he might not get a replacement due to the cost cutting exercises. Tom starts the meeting with no agenda and no boundary conditions for the discussions, but spends 20 minutes giving everyone some background information on why they are there, and makes sure everyone understands that he needs to take the best ideas to his boss within a week.

Bob finally comes into the meeting with a weak excuse for being late and disrupts the current conversation. Tom feels that everyone must be on the same page, so he backs up and spends another 15 minutes stating what has already been said so that Bob also understands.

Chandler and Shirley are always annoyed with the special treatment that Bob gets, and begin to throw out ideas. Mary is very quiet, but Shirley is especially animated today - she normally does most of the talking in the meetings when it's time to discuss a topic. No one is capturing the ideas, so Chandler decides to jump up and grab a marker at the white board. The next 45 minutes become more of a conversation between Shirley who is talking and Chandler who is trying to write things down but is having some difficulty following Shirley. Mary begins to read her e-mail and Bob is texting on his smart phone, due to something he claims is "urgent" to Sales. Brent and Larisa look at each other and with no words said, they both understood what each other was thinking. They are sitting in another meeting where no one is really in charge, and it's turning into chaos.

They take a 20-minute break because 2 people leave to go to the restroom. After resuming the meeting with only 4 people there, Shirley and Chandler begin to disagree on one of the items on the white board. This turns into a detailed discussion - Brent and Larisa try to participate, but Shirley and Chandler dominate the conversation.

Finally, Tom tries to bring some order to the discussion. He asks Chandler to write up the few ideas that are on the white board, and since he has a lunch meeting with his boss, he closes the meeting at 11:45 – almost 3 hours after the start with minimal results. Tom announces they will continue this discussion tomorrow morning at 9am.

It is easy to see that the results of this meeting were poor at best. Actually this is a fairly complicated case study with much to learn, and it may seem obvious that the meeting was a disaster, yet I've witnessed meetings of this type in a number of companies and settings.

Tom's objective was to brainstorm ideas with his team and collect the best ideas to then take to his boss. Instead, he ended up with 3 hours wasted and only a few ideas that certainly would not be ready to present. What did Tom do wrong?

As the Supervisor of the team, he set a poor example by not clearly defining the structure of the meeting and he had no facilitator, scribe or timekeeper assigned. In this case, a facilitator would make sure that no one person dominated the conversation. By doing this, the creative ideas from the new hires could have been brought to the table in addition to the ideas from those who had a lot of experience.

By announcing the agenda up front, Tom could have a timekeeper make sure that the meeting stayed on track. If a topic needed extending, this could have been a decision rather than simply allowing the meeting to take it's own undefined course dictated by those who are the loudest. Bob's tardiness would not have derailed the meeting, as an agenda with specific time sections would rule. Tom could have covered anything that Bob missed later, one-on-one, and used that time also to coach Bob that the team expects everyone to be on time out of respect for each other.

In the best examples of high performing team meetings, the team will spend significant time to form an agreement on how they will have meetings. Everyone signs the agreement in an act of unity and respect for each other.

Conversation Scorecard - Tom	Y/N	Supporting Evidence
Was the Relationship recognized?	N	Even though Tom is the supervisor, he did not establish ground rules up front or set the stage for a productive meeting.
Was the Situation recognized?	N	In this case one-to-many situation was not effectively recognized.
Was the Bridge Anchored?	N	Tom did little to make sure that all bridges were anchored. Mary became completely disengaged.
Was the Traffic Managed?	N	Another disaster. There was no facilitator, and the most aggressive people basically ran the meeting.
Was the Bridge closed appropriately?	N	Tom had lost control and simply had to end the meeting due to another commitment.
Was there a Successful Outcome?	N	The next step appears to be to get back together for more unproductive discussion. The team is frustrated.
Overall Score	0/6	**Not Successful** – This meeting did not have a successful outcome, and all steps in the process need improvement.

In this example, Tom could have also improved the situation by performing the role of a strong, but reasonable facilitator. Knowing the characteristics of his staff, he could manage multiple bridges and the traffic by drawing in the participants who were less aggressive and slowing the traffic coming from the aggressive staff members.

This is a clear example of where the supervisor who is skilled in Balance the Bridge concepts must provide strong leadership in order to balance multiple bridges.

CASE STUDY #6: POSITION-OF-AUTHORITY, ONE-TO-MANY

A Master Communicator at Work

A number of years ago, HP sponsored executive training sessions on the campus of MIT. CEOs and CIOs attended three-day sessions led by Professor John Donovan, a retired professor and entrepreneur, and a master communicator on the subject of business computing and client-server technology.

The premise was that most businesses had poor linkage between business and IT in the company, and that IT was stuck with old technology and old methodologies, essentially holding the company "hostage".

Not only was John Donovan knowledgeable about these topics, but he was also a master in communication skills and techniques. You could feel the magic in the classroom as people responded to him. They felt they were back in college, learning from a master professor. Field trips to visit the sights in Boston that are an important part of US history were woven in to the program. He emphasized youth and the future…. dreaming and hope.

These were not easy students to persuade: CEOs and CIOs from the Fortune 500. If a technical specialist had delivered the information in a more routine setting such as an office conference room, it would have been tough to even get the audience in the room. The fact that the CEOs and CIOs were "learning" on the grounds of a prestigious US university allowed them to internalize the message when traditional methods might have failed.

The method, in addition to the materials, was the "magic sauce" in preparation of a fantastic meal. I have witnessed many cases of excellence in conversations involving Position of Authority, One to Many – in some sense it is similar to magnificent art...difficult to describe, but you know it when you see it.

John Donovan is an expert at balancing the bridges between him and a large group of executives. He would take advantage of breaks and dinners to really get to know the executives and their spouses or guests when they would come on the trip also. His professor style and qualifications were emphasized during lecture, and he used demonstrations and young, talented graduate students from MIT and Harvard to make sure the lectures were full of exciting information and compelling stories that hit home with this tough audience. He allowed much time for questions and dialogue with interesting guest speakers including people like Robert Reich, who had been a professor at Harvard and the Secretary of Labor under Bill Clinton. Often Lew Platt, the HP CEO or one of our Executive VPs would attend to demonstrate HP's commitment to helping our largest customers realize the benefits of client-server computing and rapid application development.

At the time, my role at HP included functioning as one of the executive sponsors, and I typically would have my team of architects there to assist with follow up meetings to discuss how we could take what the executives had learned at the course and move the concepts forward in their company, typically through a pilot or proof of concept project. Usually I would deliver a short lecture to speak about the rapid application development methodology before John started for the day and highlight some customer examples where we had been successful.

I got to know John Donavan very well, regularly having tea with him at the Harvard Club after a dinner to talk about how to make the courses more successful. What I learned from John is that you can't teach charisma. But, given enough determination and the right process you can often develop charisma. John Kennedy, Martin Luther King Jr. and Adolf Hitler all learned this too. You must have natural skill, but also work hard on preparation and delivery.

The three simple tips in developing charisma that I learned from John are:

1) Be confident through your words and body language – this means not only being very comfortable who you are but simply showing people that you are confident through what you say and how you say it.
2) Convey high energy – people gravitate to those who are full of energy and conviction.
3) Demonstrate sincere care for people to make them feel special – the more you show people how much you care for them, the more they will gravitate to your leadership and ideas.

John understood the importance of having strong, anchored bridges with his audience. He understood that the flow of traffic and being able to use all kinds of compelling stories, demos and resources could provide an experience much different from the traditional ways of selling technology to companies. John took advantage of the historical ground we walked on and the importance of Harvard and MIT in the educational and research world. And, John was a master at managing the flow of traffic and had a sixth sense for when things were unbalanced. He could, on the fly, bring things back into balance, and in the end close the bridge so that the audience felt as though they just experienced a very valuable lecture. And, he knew that with this type of executive, tours of historic Boston that included memorable dinners and entertainment by some of the finest talent from Harvard would create the environment for them to open up and begin to talk about their environment and possibilities for the future where IT and Business would work closely together using the proposed methodologies.

An example of this is a routine we used many times. After dinner at the Harvard Club with our guests at round tables of 8, John and I would walk around the room with a glass of wine or water to each table. When we arrived at the table it was time to have a brief, but powerful peer-to-peer, one-to-few conversation. Arriving at the table we would raise the glass and give a toast, thanking those at the table for attending. Then, John would ask a great, open-ended question to the table or to a specific executive: "…What did you like most about the day?…" This would allow the executive, and ultimately multiple people at the table, to open up and share a key learning. It was a great way to end the day on a positive note and set the stage for more great things to come tomorrow.

I use this as a case study for Position-of-Authority, One-to-Many because essentially John Donavan was the professor and the executives were the students in this setting, even though they did not technically work for John. His skills were so strong that he was able to "assume" the Position of Authority.

Conversation Scorecard - John	Y/N	Supporting Evidence
Was the Relationship recognized?	Y	John set the stage appropriately as he was in position of authority.
Was the Situation recognized?	Y	John adjusted when one-to-many was the situation or when it moved to either one-to-few or one-to-one.
Was the Bridge Anchored?	Y	John was very sensitive at all times to make sure that the bridges were all anchored and he would repair any immediately if the anchor became weak.
Was the Traffic Managed?	Y	John demonstrated the ability to know when it was best to pull traffic from the class and when it was best to lecture to make sure the executives received a great experience.
Was the Bridge closed appropriately?	Y	John always summarized and made sure that next steps were clearly defined.
Was there a Successful Outcome?	Y	Class ratings were outstanding from these tough audiences. Through charisma and balancing the bridge, John generated the awareness on how to align business and technology, which was the primary goal.
Overall Score	6/6	**Successful** – These events had successful outcomes, and all steps in the process were on track!

Chapter 11

THE WORK ENVIRONMENT

After many years of planning, construction began on the Sydney Harbour Bridge in 1923. The bridge finally opened in 1932, connecting the Sydney central business district and the north shore. The bridge is a "steel through arch" bridge, a common design used in many cities around the world. In addition to being an icon of Sydney and Australia, it provides for rail, automobile, bicycle and pedestrian traffic over the Sydney Harbour. According to many sources, this bridge is nicknamed "The Coathanger" due to the arch design.

Just like the Sydney Harbour Bridge, communication bridges in the workplace may need to carry many different types of traffic. And, during the workday you may have to constantly adjust the type and pace of traffic flowing across the bridges to have the most effective conversations.

THE SYDNEY HARBOR BRIDGE

© CAN STOCK PHOTO INC. / SUNNYTIME

MEETINGS

Thousands of bridges allow people to get to work each day. I could write an entire book on the use of Balance the Bridge in the work environment, but for now, I will simply focus on a few settings where the model can be very effective. Let's begin this discussion with something that happens in almost every work situation… the "meeting".

You may be in a job now that causes you to participate in a lot of meetings. These could be customer meetings or internal meetings. And, even if your work does not include meetings, certainly you will experience meetings at places such as school, church and social clubs. I experience meetings most every day and have done so for decades. These have been customer meetings and internal meetings. Prior to technology advances there were many more face-to-face meetings in most industries.

As technology advanced it allowed more people to work at home and communicate from anywhere to anyone with cell phones or in "virtual rooms". There is still a need for face-to-face meetings and this will likely never go away. However, with the rise in "virtual" meetings, new skills and new approaches are required.

Meetings require a special focus on balance. As I indicated earlier, I learned in one situation that my management team was not working together well, especially in meetings. Once balance was established, the overall team performance went up drastically.

A common version of a meeting today is known as the conference call. Virtually all businesses can have conference calls at very low cost and it's a good way to have a meeting with people who are not necessarily in the same physical office.

I can remember my first job in the hi-tech industry – we had corded phones at a desk and no voicemail. There was no e-mail and when you called someone from the road, you stopped at a pay phone along the side of the road. Sometimes, I would stop at a hotel and look for the magic bank of phones against a wall outside of the conference rooms and I would pull up a chair to make a series of phone calls. When I was out for the day with customers, my assistant would take messages on a pink pad that said "While you were out" at the top of the message. There was a blank line for her to write in the name of the person and then that individual's phone number and the basic message or reason for the call. All of the correspondence and proposals were done on a typewriter and I would take my best pen and sign letters every day.

Today, of course, we have cell phones, e-mail, texting, social media and many other ways to stay connected. Certainly, a technology improvement that has increased the ability for many people to interact is the proliferation of the conference call.

And, more and more, video conference calling is being used that allows at least some level of visual interaction similar to the face-to-face meeting.

Regardless of whether your meeting is face-to-face or via conference call, there are a few techniques that should be used to improve the balance and success of each meeting.

> *Begin with an agenda that is time bound.*

An agenda that is time bound is a critical step to make sure that you start out with a defined list of topics and timeframe for each topic. It doesn't mean that things can't change, but a change in topic or time for a topic needs to be a conscious decision by the leader, or team, if the leader allows the team to make this type of decision.

> *Secondly, always have at least 4 specific roles assigned to people in the meeting. These four are facilitator, timekeeper, scribe and content provider.*

Defining at least four roles, including facilitator, time keeper, scribe and content provider is another best practice.

The facilitator's job is to initiate the topic by establishing the bridge. They then manage the traffic to make sure that bridges stay anchored and traffic flows appropriately. The timekeeper's job is to keep the facilitator informed on how much time is left that has been assigned to this particular topic.

Should the timekeeper choose to provide content in the meeting or ask questions, they must announce they are stepping out of their role briefly and then return to their role as soon as they have finished supplying the content or received the answer to their question. Timekeeping is their #1 priority. The scribe is there to capture important discussion points, decisions made and actions to be taken based upon the discussion. The scribe may provide content or ask a question only if they announce they are stepping out of their role to do so – then they return to their role just as the timekeeper must do.

Content providers present materials or ask questions. Basically, these people are the people who are either informing others on a topic or in need of the information in order to make decisions or take action. Content providers typically don't take on any other role. Finally, the facilitator must stay in role unless announcing that he or she is stepping out of the role.

The facilitator should always cover the meeting ground rules at the beginning of the meeting. It's wise for the facilitator to confirm these rules with the person in position of authority first to make sure he has support. I've seen facilitators get embarrassed by launching into meeting ground rules, only to be dismissed in the first 15 minutes by the ranking executive in the meeting.

Improving team meetings can be complex, but the above guidelines have been proven to improve the balance and ultimately help to generate very productive, high performing teams. Custom team analysis and information

> *A best practice for ground rules is to establish agreement on how questions will be handled, and how the group will decide to either end a topic if time runs out or if they are willing to sacrifice other topics.*

on workshops can be found on balancethebridge.com (another shameless plug!)

PRESENTATIONS

It's hard to find a work environment in this day and age that does not include the "dreaded Windows PowerPoint or Mac Keynote presentation". If you are not familiar with these software products, they essentially allow the presenter to create pages for presentations that can be put up on a screen or printed out for the audience. There are entire books written on how to give effective presentations using PowerPoint or Keynote. In this case, I will point out key best practices as it relates to the ability to Balance the Bridge between the presenter and the audience, be it a few people or a very large group.

Remember, that when giving a presentation at work, you must make sure you continue to have the bridge anchored between you and the audience when delivering the message. In this day and age, it is all too common (yet still rude) for people to have cell phones and laptops on during work presentations.

It's even worse if you are delivering a presentation on a conference call because you can't even make eye contact with your audience. You can almost always be guaranteed that at least some in the audience will be multi-tasking during your presentation, and unless your message is compelling, the bridge will not be anchored on their side very quickly.

Unless the audience is just a few people who know the topic very well and are asking and expecting a lot of detail you should:

1) Keep the slides very simple, using perhaps a size 28 pt font or larger.

2) Keep the text in bullets (phrases rather than full sentences) and verbally give more information – basically tell a story to the audience.

3) Many sources talk about using the "rule of 3" here, and I agree. A good rule of 3 for the overall presentation would be Current State of the Situation, Desired State of the Situation, How We are Going to Get There.

4) No more than 10 slides max and no more than 20 minutes of presentation – most meetings allow for 45min to 1 hour for a topic, and allowing for plenty of discussion time makes the presentation much more effective.

5) Pictures, charts, graphs, illustrations are generally much better than text on the slides. Studies have shown that we learn and retain more from visual images than from text.

Example of a Poor Slide – Too "Wordy"

- Keep the slides very simple, using perhaps a size 28 pt font or larger.
- Keep the text in bullets (phrases rather than full sentences) and
- verbally give more information – basically tell a story to the audience
- Many sources talk about using the "rule of 3" here, and I agree. A good
- rule of 3 for the overall presentation would be Current State, Desired State
- of the Situation, How We are Going to Get There.
- No more than 10 slides max and no more than 20 minutes of presentation -
- most meetings allow for 45 min to 1 hour for a topic, and allowing plenty
- of discussion time makes the presentation much more effective.
- Pictures, charts, graphs, illustrations are generally much better than text
- on the slides. Studies have shown that we learn and retain more from
- visual images than from text.

Example of a Good Slide

- Use a large font
- Keep text in bullet form
- Use the Rule of 3
  - Current State
  - Desired State
  - How We Will Get There
- 10 slides max – allow time for discussion
- Use Pictures and Illustrations when possible

Now that you have a good architecture for your next presentation, the key thing to remember is to pay close attention to the bridge and make sure you manage the traffic. The best way to do this is to pause briefly during the presentation and check for understanding. You must be careful with this as some attendees might take over the presentation, but if you test the concepts in advance with a few key people, you can then use them as support during the presentation.

> *I learned over the years that you almost always have a winning presentation if you can turn data into information that can drive action.*

Also, it's a good practice to have backup materials that contain more detail when you get the question from the person demanding more data on some topic. Remember the objective of the presentation – the larger the audience gets, the simpler the slides should be, with your verbal story giving the succinct details that support the statements on the slides.

There are many good reference books on how to deliver effective presentations. 3 of my favorites are:

1) Presentation Zen by Garr Reynolds
2) How to Deliver a TED talk by Jeremy Donovan, and
3) slide: ology by Nancy Duarte

Reading these books and others can really help you to have winning presentations in almost any environment. And, remember that while delivering your message you should establish and maintain a strong, anchored bridge between you and the audience.

There are many more examples of how to use Balance the Bridge in the work environment. I plan to focus on these in greater detail in my next book.

Now, let's look at some additional evidence from everyday life that balance is extremely important for success.

Chapter 12

FINDING EXAMPLES OF BALANCE IN LIFE

The Millau Viaduct opened in 2004 in Southern France. As with many bridges that are built, it was designed to reduce traffic problems. In this case, there was significant traffic congestion along the roads near Millau through the Tarn Valley during the holiday season as travelers would go from Paris to Spain and back. There were four possible routes for the bridge, but three of them posed significant challenges and in the end the best route was chosen, but it was going to set a record.

At 2460m in total length, it is the world's tallest bridge with one mast's summit at 343m (1125 feet) above the base of the structure. That's taller than the Eiffel tower – a sight to behold!

The architects of the Millau Viaduct had to balance the challenges of building the tallest bridge in the world with the other possible route challenges. As you examine many areas in life, you discover the importance of balance.

THE MILLAU VIADUCT

To illustrate how balance plays a key role in everyday life, I've decided to cover three areas that are very important to me, and many others: Music, Cooking and Exercise.

THE NEED FOR BALANCE IN MUSIC

I happen to love music... almost all types of music... and music gives us some significant examples related to this topic.

Music is often called "the universal language". A "bridge" is used in many types of music, generally referring to a piece or section that provides transition between two parts of the song or composition.

It doesn't matter if the music is classical from the 1600s, big band tunes of the 1940s, rock and roll from the 1970s or even popular music today, it is critical to balance all of the parts. Magic occurs in the musical mix when you can hear all of the voices and instruments.

At times, a particular voice or instrument needs to "dominate", but in general, balance is crucial and often the sound engineers are charged with making sure everyone can be heard in the mix. In conversations, the same is true. Balance is critical and you can be the sound engineer. Others may not understand this concept, but if you keep this in mind and use techniques to achieve the balance, the result can also be magic.

Imagine that your child is on stage with a group of musicians and singers and she has a solo vocal during the song. Then, instead of hearing her, the microphone is not working and you hear nothing of her solo. You would be frustrated, upset and maybe even angry. During conversations and dialogue, the same needs to be true. If you understand the need for balance then you can attempt to encourage it, create it and even manage it.

I've been a musician for over 45 years – something that began around age 8 during my first piano lesson. Like many young musicians, I became fascinated to hear how multiple notes could be combined, in tune, to provide simple chords, and then I began learning that there were countless possibilities in the world of music.

Not only were their many things to learn on one instrument...then by combining various instruments you could get very different sounds. After combining different instruments, distinct patterns in the music could produce a "style" of music. It might even be the same instruments, but you could get classical, jazz, pop, rock, blues and the list goes on and on.

Then I got very interested in how the various musical parts of a song could be mixed and blended. I bought my first mixer decades ago and taught myself how to become the sound engineer by learning from those who were experts at this. Having a degree in Electrical Engineering and also growing up as a musician meant I would be fascinated with technology that began with simple amplification and has led to computer based digital audio workstations and incredible hardware and software that is commonly used today to produce the music that the whole world listens to.

Much of my musical life has been performing in groups – and, I have been fortunate to play an instrument and sing in a variety of settings. Early in life I was in many groups at our church in Louisville, KY including choirs and ensembles. School opportunities included marching band and orchestras plus an opportunity while in High School to play in a USO type band that would entertain the troops at Ft. Knox.

One Sunday a month we would board the bus and drive to Ft. Knox where 5000 troops were ready to hear big band music and listen to a group sing and dance. This was in contrast to perhaps the previous Friday night when my bluegrass band was playing at a party or just jamming at someone's house. It was the mid-70s and of course we had Motown, rock 'n roll, disco – you name it, the musical possibilities seemed endless. I was hooked. Music was part of my blood as my parents encouraged it, and my grandfather who lived to be 103 was even playing his guitar with me when he was 100 years old!

Balance means being able to hear all the parts of the song. Balance means being able to get the right sound out of the group of instrumentalists and vocalists. Balance also means harmony – the type that could give you chills. Balance means fans are happy. Balance means all the musicians are happy. A lack of balance means the opposite. Unhappy fans, unhappy musicians or vocalists, and it just does not sound right.

> So, I grew up playing and singing everything from Baptist hymns to bluegrass to rock and roll, but when I began mixing I learned that there was definitely one thing good music had in common no matter what type it was – there was a need for balance.

For some reason, most people don't understand the need for balance in conversations. They don't understand that without the proper balance, conversations and relationships never reach their full potential. As a matter of fact, a lack of proper balance can often mean that conversations fail and relationships sour. People often are confused and simply don't understand why problems exist – or, they simply blame the other party when the right move is to examine their skills and methods of communicating.

As I sit and write this section of the book, I am fortunate enough to be at the Grove Park Inn in Asheville, NC overlooking the Blue Ridge mountains. In the lobby, I am listening to 2 wonderful classical guitar players who are on the faculty of nearby Brevard College in Brevard, North Carolina. One of the things that is so wonderful about this pair is the balance in their playing. They understand exactly how to adjust the volume and pace with each other so that the music sounds as one musician. They seem connected to each other and they manage the traffic of musical notes flowing from each instrument so that a wonderful balance is achieved. Talented musicians grasp balance and how critical it is to pay attention to create the best possible feeling and experience for the audience.

The next time you listen to one of your favorite songs, pay close attention to the balance across voices and instruments. Then, start thinking about conversations in this light!

COOKING – ANOTHER GOOD EXAMPLE!

I am a self-proclaimed Food Network addict and I absolutely love to cook. The more I watch people cook and the more I try new things, the more I am fascinated with it. As I type this on a flight high above the ground half way from Atlanta to San Francisco, I have the Food Network on the in-flight entertainment system, so it must be appropriate that I write this case study at this time.

Of course, engineers can be dangerous cooks – they often like lots and lots of data… the more data, the better. What are the ingredients? What is the sequence of preparation? What are the variables of success? Temperature required? Time of cooking?

To get a good dose of this just go to cookingforengineers.com and you will see what I mean. Of course, all good cooks know that recipes are most often the guide to success until you've got a lot of experience with a particular dish…. Then, you can just cook it with no recipe on hand because you have the experience. And, if you are a cook like me, you unfortunately have made quite a few mistakes along the way, but there is just a special feeling when cooking a dish that turns out right and makes your family or friends happy.

I've also been fortunate to travel to most every state in the US and many countries outside of the US – the variety of food seems endless. To me, just the variety of ingredients, the endless methods of cooking and local traditions are simply fascinating.

Whether it is Nuremburg Sausages in the center of town in Nuremburg, Germany or a Fried Shrimp Po-Boy in the French Quarter of New Orleans or a cup of Burgoo in horse country at Keeneland in Lexington, KY – there are cooks with wonderful talents and a tremendous blend of ingredients everywhere. There are many things that good cooks have in common – certainly one thing is the ability to balance the recipe with the right amount of each ingredient to reach the taste they are after.

One day when I was cooking a soup in a slow cooker, I began thinking how important it is to have the right balance of ingredients – about that time I witnessed a conversation that was way out of balance. It was so clear to me that this was like having way too much salt in the soup... or like missing a key ingredient from the recipe. The soup still gets made, and perhaps people will still eat it, but it would be so much better with the right balance.

Conversations are the same way, and every day they happen out of balance. People still keep talking, and things keep getting done, but the interaction would be so much better and productive with the right balance. If you are a cook, either fulltime or just as needed, try to think about conversations as a soup. Balance the ingredients, and balance the conversation.

EXERCISE

Exercise has always been important to me. Growing up, I played all kinds of sports, settling in on soccer as my favorite sport in high school and college. I was proud to be a team captain in both high school and college – probably my "type A" personality led me to want to lead and inspire others on the soccer field. I never thought much about staying in shape as I had a pretty high metabolism and was pretty thin.

Once I graduated from college, got married and went to work for HP, I was traveling and eating out with customers rather than running up and down the soccer field. This, of course, led to a few extra pounds and before too long I realized that an exercise routine would be important. Then in 1982, I suddenly started losing weight at an alarming rate for no apparent reason. At the same time, I had an incredible thirst and remember drinking an entire 6 pack of soft drinks at the office one afternoon.

Knowing something was not right, I went to the doctor, and was told that I had developed type-one diabetes. This particular type is also known as juvenile diabetes, which was a surprise to me as I was in my 20s. But, apparently many people develop type-one diabetes even after they are grown, and I was one of them.

I quickly learned that this would be a life long condition, but the good news was that it could be managed. Juvenile diabetes means that the pancreas has stopped producing insulin or doesn't produce enough to handle the process of turning blood sugar into energy for the cells in your body. Instead, the blood sugar remains high if more insulin is not introduced, and thus this type of diabetes requires regular insulin injections.

I was surprised how quickly I got used to giving myself injections and to this day it doesn't really bother me at all. More importantly, the advancement in insulin treatment over the past few decades and advancement in monitoring blood sugar has created a situation where diabetics can do very well and be very healthy, if they simply observe and practice some key processes.

As a matter of fact, if you have diabetes and follow the guidelines today, you will live a healthier lifestyle than most Americans who don't have the condition. It boils down to…you guessed it…balance! To be healthy, diabetics must balance the food they eat with insulin they take and an appropriate amount of exercise. Essentially it is a "three-legged stool" where if all three legs are appropriate the stool remains stable and the blood sugar remains in the normal range, which is between 80 and 120 milligrams of sugar per deciliter of blood. Diabetics learn how to count carbohydrates and learn how much insulin is required against what they are consuming to keep the blood sugar in the good range.

Now, I mentioned exercise, and this is key – not only for diabetics, but also for everyone. Obesity, defined as a body mass index > 30kg/m^2, has been steadily increasing in the US since the 1980s according to the Journal of the American Medical Association.[12]

Much of this is due to a dangerous trend of Americans consuming more and exercising less. And, it's no secret that being either overweight or obese leads to many illnesses and health challenges. As a diabetic, I learned early on the importance of exercise as one of the three legs on the stool. Then, I learned that there was another stool to consider with three legs to be balanced.

Personal trainers and fitness experts will tell you that to be in great shape you need to balance three things: Aerobic exercise, resistance exercise and the fuel (food) you put in the body. By having good balance in each one of these areas, you can be in great physical shape. I've been able to maintain excellent blood sugar readings and good weight control by simply making sure the balance

---

[12] www.jama.jamanetwork.com, Retrieved 10-23-13, http://jama.jamanetwork.com/article.aspx?articleid=192036

is appropriate. Yet another good example of the importance of balance!

There are countless additional areas in life where balance is critical to success...I've simply cited a few for illustration. You need to internalize that communications is simply one of those areas that gets better with balance!

Chapter 13

BEWARE OF TECHNOLOGY

The Big Four Bridge across the Ohio River at Louisville, KY was originally built in 1895 and updated in 1929. It was built to accommodate rail traffic from what was known at the time as the Big Four Railroad, which was a nickname for the Cleveland, Cincinnati, Chicago and St. Louis Railway.

However, use declined in the mid-1960s as railroads began to merge and rail traffic was re-routed. Sources indicate that by 1969, both approach spans had been removed and sold for scrap. I was growing up in Louisville at the time, and I remember seeing the bridge often thinking that no one could use it anymore...it was known as "the bridge to nowhere".

It remained that way for decades, until just recently it re-opened as a pedestrian bridge. It now is a great example of how creative minds can adapt even old, worn out useless things and give them new life.

I took this photo of the bridge from the Kentucky side before the pedestrian access was completed. If you look closely you can see how the bridge has no connection on the Indiana side. It looked like this for decades. It was an icon for me when thinking of communication bridges that are not anchored. Technology has ironically made it more difficult at times to anchor the bridge.

THE BIG FOUR BRIDGE

Everything that can be invented has been invented.

- *Charles H. Duell, Commissioner U.S. Patent Office 1899*

The above quote is a great example of how you should never assume that things in place today will not change. Heraclitus, the Greek philosopher who lived around 500 B.C. is credited for the quote: "...the only thing constant is change...". And, as life around us changes we must adapt.

Just think of examples of things invented after Charles Duell made that statement... radio and television, the automobile and the airplane, air conditioning and penicillin, the transistor (which may be the most significant invention of the 20ᵗʰ century) that led to modern day electronics including cell phones, PCs, tablets and the list goes on.

THE PROBLEM

Beware of Technology would seem to be a strange chapter coming from an electrical engineer who worked for over 30 years for what is now one of the largest technology companies in the world. However, let's examine what has happened in recent decades…

As mentioned, for only the past 100 years have we had such things as electricity, telephones, televisions and automobiles. This means that for thousands of years, mankind lived without such devices… so, what does that have to do with communication? Essentially, everyone did a lot more talking and listening before all of this technology was invented – good, solid communication before technology was a critical a part of our lives. Most families used to have significant dinner conversations. A good friend of mine, Jeff Ramminger, a Senior VP at Tech Target, recently told me how he was in a restaurant and watched a family of four spend the entire time with no conversation because everyone was fooling around with their smart phone. Not a single word was said while they were dining. Jeff is a brilliant IT Executive, and we agree that this is a very sad situation.

People used to visit each other and sit on the porch just to talk with no television involved. Then, when telephones came along, they were still mostly used for conversations instead of texting, photos, e-mail and internet access. Even as I write this chapter, I am using a laptop on an airplane instead of having a conversation with the person sitting right beside me.

The end result is that people can go through their entire day now and not even have a face-to-face conversation with anyone. In a sense, the "art" of conversation is rapidly becoming a lost art. And, every day I see a major mistake made when people are in fact having a face-to-face conversation. They allow their technology to take priority over their face-to-face conversation.

CELL PHONES

How many times have you been talking to someone when their cell phone rings and they answer the phone. This immediately sends the message that the cell phone call is more important than the face-to-face conversation.

Another example is the text message interruption… the phone beeps signaling a new text message and suddenly reading and answering it becomes the top priority. *I actually promote that the opposite should be true.*

> *If you are having a conversation with someone and your phone rings or beeps, you should simply apologize to the person you am talking to that it even made a sound, and look at it after the conversation is over to see who called. This sends the message that your face-to-face conversation is the top priority right now.*

Alternatively, you could ask the person if it is OK if you answer, but only if you also speak to a situation that would make sense to allow an interruption.

A good example of this would be where you are having a conversation with a good friend and your cell phone rings and you then say – I'm sorry – would you mind if I answer this? – my father has been sick and I think this may be him calling.

In that quick moment, you have let your friend know that there is an extenuating circumstance.

Your friend most likely would not feel slighted but would understand the interruption. Your friend could perhaps relate to the situation and think that they would do the same thing if a family member was ill. The critical part is asking permission rather than just answering the phone, putting your face-to-face conversation "on hold". I have never met a person who enjoys being put on hold. I have met plenty of people who despise being put on hold. Unless you know the person very, very well, you can't be sure how they feel about being put "on hold".

Don't allow technology to put your live conversations "on hold" or you may find that the bridge will be severed either for this conversation, or worst case, forever.

E-MAIL

In the 1980s, electronic mail now known as e-mail rose to prominence. In offices around the world, no longer were you forced to type a memo or call a meeting – you could compose an electronic mail message and send it to one person or many in an electronic distribution list. All of a sudden, in many situations you could be much more productive. Then along came voice mail, and the concept of voice mail distribution lists. I lived through this transition in business and noticed a very interesting phenomenon.

Conversations decreased. One-way communications increased. Sometimes, conversations that used to occur over an hour instead went on for weeks over e-mail exchanges. And, when you would send someone an e-mail or leave them a voicemail, you could say whatever you wanted without them discussing it with you, at least right away. *So, e-mail and voice mail became a way for some people to avoid conversations.* I recall cases where people were in the same office but instead of having a conversation they would send e-mail and voice mail to people sometimes sitting at the desk next to them.

> *Don't use technology to avoid having a conversation. Instead, use technology to enhance your conversations.*

Instead of conversation avoidance, use technology for conversation enhancement. Most people enjoy a follow up e-mail to a conversation. It could simply confirm what you understood from the dialogue or even thank them for spending the time with you. It can give you an opportunity to give more detail on the topic being discussed if they so choose to be interested.

SOCIAL MEDIA AND GOOD MANNERS

However, no technology allows you to really develop the kind of relationship that can be developed face to face. There is no body language, no handshake or hug. My favorite example now is the social networking applications like Facebook and Twitter. We seem to be developing an entire new generation of people who tweet and text their way to conversations with followers and tell their daily story to their friends on Facebook, or using some other app on their smart phone.

I don't mean to imply that these technologies are bad for you, or that they should be avoided all together. However, if you suddenly become a person who spends the majority of your time communicating through these methods, you will never be able to develop your face-to-face communication skills to the extent that they can be developed.

It certainly appears that the ability to use mobile technology is going to continue to increase with better, faster hardware and software plus ever more network bandwidth and speed. This will most certainly result in mobile multi-media application improvement and essentially the ability to interact with many, many things just by using a "smart, mobile device".

My prediction is that live conversations will continue to suffer. The skills of the young will not be forced to develop until the smart ones realize the importance of having good conversational skills. But then, the ability to develop these skills will be reduced due to the increasing use of technology and the increase of the numbers of people who do not possess the skills. Essentially we are creating an entire generation of people who have limited conversational skills. So, if you develop your communication skills, you'll have the potential to stand out as a great communicator.

A ray of hope, however, is the fact that many people are beginning to understand this phenomenon, and are beginning to take much greater care when using technology. Another bi-product of technology is an overall reduction in good manners.

I can remember as if it was yesterday when I was growing up being taught that it is bad manners to interrupt someone. Even "professionals" on national television today make it a habit to interrupt each other while on the air! There seems to be a simple expectation that interrupting someone in mid-sentence is not only acceptable, but even considered appropriate...

Whatever happened to good manners and listening before you talk? In an interrupting environment, the loudest, most aggressive person typically dominates the conversation.

As this becomes a fundamental expectation of how people communicate, it obviously can and does spill over into conversations in the home. Spouses interrupting each other, children and parents interrupting each other, friends interrupting each other... at best the traffic across the bridge turns into a disorganized traffic jam or at worst the bridge dissolves and traffic never makes it to the other side.

Even worse is people interrupting each other and assuming this is "just the way it is" and the proper way to communicate. Essentially, they are accepting that living in a traffic jam all of the time is just fine and the way it should be. I don't know about you, but I hate traffic jams. I love it when traffic flows smoothly in a conversation. I learn the most when I am not talking. I help people most to develop when they actively listen and ask good questions based upon what they learn in the conversation.

A GENERATIONAL ISSUE

An experiment that I have done over the past several years involves observing the different way that generations of people communicate with each other. I have analyzed hundreds of conversations involving dozens of people 70 years old and over. The same goes for the group currently ages 35 – 70 and the age group under 35 today. The findings are fascinating.

> On average, the skills of the age group currently 70 years old and older far exceed the conversation skills of the group currently 35 and younger. The age group currently 35 – 70 is a mixed bag of skills.

My theory is that the age group who is now 70 years and older grew up in a time where conversational skills were not only encouraged, but required. There were no cell phones, internet, TV, beepers and those who were role models would exhibit good manners and excellent communication skills. Therefore, it was only natural to try to develop these kinds of skills.

The age group currently under 35 has in fact grown up in an age filled with technology and different expectations of what is considered good communication skills. Interrupting a live conversation to take a cell phone call seems perfectly acceptable to many. Interrupting another person to take over the conversation is not only common, it is seen in some circles as a skill.

So-called "Reality TV" is a great example of this. From this perspective, reality TV is simply a demonstration that showing no manners or skills is now a reality and even worth watching on TV. Real Housewives, Jersey Shore – you name it – watch one of these shows and try to find any possible example of good communication skills.

Now, that said, there are certainly many examples of people under 35 who have great communication skills and are very talented when it comes to balancing the bridge. These people are to be commended as the world around them is not currently encouraging the attainment of this skill. The world has simply accepted "information overload" as a norm including chaos in conversations.

I mentioned that the group currently 35 – 70 is a mixed bag. I believe this to be true because many of them grew up in environments where manners and skills were encouraged and taught. And, some have retained this and even taken it to the next level of skill. But, many in this group have also allowed the current practices of technology and information overload to dictate how they communicate today – basically saying: Get over it – the world has changed. I would submit that while the world has certainly changed, the need for good communication skills has never been greater.

Bottom line: Continue to learn and embrace all forms of new technology… but never let technology replace the importance of good, face-to-face communication skills. And, recognize that it will simply become more difficult to master good communication skills as technology continues to advance.

> You will separate yourself from the masses if you develop and demonstrate good manners and excellent communication skills while also being assertive and confident. The five step Balance the Bridge process can help you do this.

As we now move to the chapter on action, consider the following quote:

> If you take too long in deciding what to do with your life, you'll find you've done it.
> George Bernard Shaw 1856 – 1950

Chapter 14

DEVELOP AND IMPLEMENT THE ACTION PLAN

The Pont du Gard is a Roman aqueduct bridge that crosses the Gardon river. Built in the 1st century A.D., it is a masterpiece in southern France. The bridge consists of 3 tiers of arches standing almost 50 meters high, making it the highest Roman construction in the world.[13]

In order to supply water to the Roman colony at Nimes, a 50 km aqueduct was built from Uzes to Nimes. The aqueduct took a long, winding route, mostly underground, but at one point had to cross the gorge of the Gardon river and it was determined that a bridge would be the best solution.

It is estimated that the aqueduct supplied the city of about 50,000 people with 44M gallons of water per day! In order to have the proper gradient, the engineers determined that the bridge would need to be 160 feet above the river. Then, 50,000 tons of nearby limestone was used to build the bridge, largely without the use of

---

[13] www.pontdugard.fr, Retrieved 10-21-13, http://www.pontdugard.fr/en/pont-du-gards-second-life

mortar or clamps. Amazing… and they didn't even have the use of a calculator, much less the internet!

THE PONT DU GARD

My hope is that you don't simply read this book, but that you internalize the concepts and take action to improve your communication skills. The Romans had detailed plans for building successful bridges. Likewise, you need a plan for building and balancing your communication bridges. Let's take a look at best practices in developing plans and then specifics on what you can d together.

INTRODUCTION TO PLANNING METHODOLOGIES

One of the things I enjoy about my profession is that I get to focus on "excellence in execution" in addition to "creating the plan for success". I call this "Operational Excellence". Some see this as being able to take a vision and mission of an organization and turn it into a plan with goals and objectives that can be executed, measured and communicated throughout the organization.

There are countless planning methodologies and I've used many of them. HP's 10 step Planning Methodology was considered a best practice for years and is still in use today by many organizations. Hoshin Planning is also one of my favorites. This methodology was developed in Japan in the 1950s and utilizes a seven-step process and a standard set of reports called Hoshin tables. Also in the 1950s, Dr. W. Edwards Deming made popular his four-step management methodology called PDCA or Plan, Do, Check, Act.

The concept is to begin by establishing the objectives and processes necessary to deliver the targeted outcome (Plan). Next, you implement the plan (Do). Next you study the results of the implementation (Check). Finally you analyze the difference between the results and the expected outcome. Adjust the plan appropriately to minimize the difference (Act), and repeat the cycle.

In the last 20 years, something called Six Sigma has become very popular. Developed by Motorola in the 1980s, Six Sigma is a set of strategies, techniques and tools for process improvement. Many companies and organizations use a version of it today, as Jack Welch was very successful using it at GE in the mid-1990s.

The improvement cycle in Six Sigma is often expressed as DMAIC, which stands for Define, Measure, Analyze, Improve and Control. I've been involved in a number of Six Sigma projects as a Six Sigma Champion – some of the projects have been successful and some not so successful. Part of the philosophy of Six Sigma is to create a special group of people in the organization who are experts in the methods. These people are often called yellow belts, green belts and black belts, and there are certification programs to achieve the various levels.

> I found that the most successful Six Sigma experts in my organization were the experts that not only knew the methodology well, but also had the best communication skills and could Balance the Bridge.

Planning and process improvement experts often forget that they frequently are dealing with people that despise formal processes and the discipline required to follow a methodology.

My recommendation to improve your communication skills with this model is to use the 4-step cycle invented by Deming – Plan, Do, Check, Act. It's simple to understand and very appropriate in this case.

To create the plan, we need to know the desired outcome, the current state, the gap and SMART goals to reduce the gap. SMART stands for Specific, Measurable, Attainable, Relevant and Time-Bound. Unless the goals you establish can pass the "SMART" test, they are not well defined.

CREATE THE PLAN

Well, enough about methodologies – let's move on to how you create your own specific plan. Earlier in the book, I spoke of something called "poor communication denial". Unfortunately, this is a very common thing. It is likely that the most difficult thing for you to do in this process will be to admit and embrace that you can improve. Even the best communicators can improve. Unless you admit and embrace this fact, you will get absolutely nothing out of this book.

If you are able to admit and embrace the need to improve, this becomes simply an exercise in how to improve. The answer is based upon the assessment described in Chapter 7 on applying the model.

Let's review the suggestions for assessment:

a. Ask others about you – use the Personal Assessment Scorecard in the appendix.
b. Start with family members or friends – ask them how they really feel about your communication skills. Do they think it is easy to talk to you or difficult? Seek open, honest feedback and tell them no matter what the response is, you will not get angry – you are trying to learn what people really think.
c. Discuss the topic with co-workers. Tell them you are trying to improve, and you would like them to describe honestly how they feel about having a conversation with you.
d. Ask someone you trust as a mentor, pastor, doctor, etc. – basically someone you trust to give you open and honest feedback.

Summarize the findings on the Personal Assessment Scorecard and look for trends – often single data points are of little value but trends can be extremely valuable – and remember that perception IS reality.

You may get more honest feedback if the information can be collected anonymously.

Enlist the help of a friend or co-worker to collect the information, making sure that those giving feedback understand that you will only get the feedback and no specifics on the origin of the feedback.

Once you have completed the Personal Assessment Scorecard, which is also known as the Current State, it's time to develop what we will call the Desired State. And, if this methodology is to be applied to a team, you can read more about assessment services on balancethebridge.com.

EXAMPLE PLAN

Let's look at an example plan. If in the assessment, you have trends to suggest that you don't listen very well, and you often dominate conversations by talking, a sample plan might include:

Desired State

I am viewed by friends, family and co-workers as someone with excellent, balanced communication skills. My communication skills become one of my greatest assets in life.

Current State

I am viewed by friends, family and co-workers as someone who does not listen very well, and often dominates conversations. My communication skills are holding me back in relationships and in my career.

Gap

In order to reach the desired state, I must reduce or eliminate the perception that I dominate conversations.

SMART Goals

1) Use Balance the Bridge over the next 6 months with 3 close friends to manage even traffic during conversations, and take advantage of reflective listening to drive the change in perception. Measure success by performing a new assessment at the end of the 6-month period with these 3 people.

2) Sit down at work with my boss and describe the current state and my desire to improve communication skills. Seek opportunities to be a facilitator in meetings that will allow me to use Balance the Bridge. Gain agreement from boss and at least 2 other co-workers to specifically observe my communication skills in the next 6 months as I use Balance the Bridge. Measure success by performing an assessment with these 3 people at the end of 6 months.

3) Have a conversation with spouse or significant other and explain my desire to improve my communication skills. Specifically, tell them I plan to reduce the perception that I

dominate conversations. Use Balance the Bridge and at the end of significant conversations over the next 6 months, ask if the traffic seemed balanced or if I am still dominating the conversation. Measure success by asking this person for feedback after 6 months – accept whatever the perception is without becoming defensive.

Now that we have the above 3 goals, we simply execute them over the next 6 months (Do). Built into these SMART goals we then assess at the end of 6 months (Check), and based upon the results we then update the current state vs. the desired state (Act).

For some, the above will seem straightforward and for others this will seem like a foreign language from outer space. The most important part of planning, and most difficult, is to actually take the next step and use the concepts learned to improve. Joel Barker, a very successful business author is credited for saying:

> *Don't just understand the concepts in Balance the Bridge. Put them into action!*

"Vision without action is merely a dream. Action without vision just passes the time. Vision with action can change the world."

Additional information on assessment services and plan development can be found on balancethebridge.com.

Chapter 15

FINAL THOUGHTS

I guess I should warn you, if I turn out to be particularly clear, you've probably misunderstood what I've said.

- *Alan Greenspan, Chairman of US Federal Reserve*

I love the above quote, as it is very thought provoking. You can read it over and over and not be quite sure what Alan was trying to say, but I think he meant to convey that his topic is so complex that it's never clear when you actually understand it.

Communications can be the same way. And, unlike things that are absolute, good conversations are qualitative in nature – they are hard to measure and most of the time the success depends on how those who had the conversation "feel" about the experience. I've tried to describe a process that can help make sure that others feel good about the conversations you have with them.

CLIMBING THE MOUNTAIN

A few years ago I had the pleasure of meeting a fascinating number of individuals from a company called Peak Teams. They are in the business of helping teams in companies engage, align and execute. Using simulations that force people to work together in teams, their clients learn the importance of commitment, how to make tough decisions and most importantly the ingredients for working as a team to achieve stretch goals.

One of the members of Peak Teams is Rex Pemberton. Rex climbed Mount Everest at a young age and he has some fascinating stories on what he went through to accomplish this goal.

Climbers must work together as a team, connected together by a climbing rope that comes into play if a climber slips or falls. There is a balance in the team as they move from one goal to the next. And, as they climb, they must create bridges to get from one location to another – most often these bridges are created with ladders that they carry throughout the climb. Nature and the natural ice on the mountain create the gaps that mean ladder bridges must be erected, then the climbers have to have the desire to cross the bridge, ever though it can be quite scary.

Their fundamental process is to first build the bridge, make sure it is well anchored on both sides and then move across it. Arguably, the emphasis in this situation is the anchor of the bridge on both sides. However, once the anchor is definitely secure, the traffic can begin, but not until this happens.

LADDER BRIDGE USED IN MOUNTAIN CLIMBING

Excellent communicators pay specific attention to the process of anchoring the bridge. And, they adjust if the bridge anchors fail. They reduce or stop traffic and go back to work on the bridge. It, after all, is the foundation for traffic. It must be firmly constructed and in place or traffic can't flow in either direction. Such is the case with conversation.

Every single day I witness conversations flowing where there is no anchored bridge, or where there is a weak or failing bridge. Sometimes I want to yell out "save the traffic!"... it's as if I can see the words and sentences falling off of the end of the bridge not anchored to their "death", never to be seen again.

Of course, the one talking can continue to effortlessly generate yet more traffic that never makes it to the other side, basically causing a mass genocide of words and sentences. In really disastrous situations, entire paragraphs and even chapters meet their demise.

Not only do the members of Peak Teams understand and communicate all of the fundamentals, they are also masters in balancing the bridge. Each team member strives to anchor the appropriate bridge and then manage the traffic across the bridge. They do this in their delivery to their client and also between each other in conducting the seminar or workshop.

INCENTIVE TO CHANGE

I wish to leave you with a concept that I will call "Incentive to Change". Sadly, even though many people will understand these concepts and agree that this is common sense, they will not change. Much of this has to do with no "Incentive to Change". Before you can apply these principles or teach them to others, you must have "Incentive to Change".

The person who starts a diet on New Years Day has incentive to change because they want to look better in the mirror or feel better about their health. This would be the result of changing their behavior and eating a better diet day in and day out. Of course we all know that most people make a decision to not continue with the diet after a short period of time.

The "Incentive to Change" sometimes is not as great as the negative forces pulling them back into their old ways. Another example of low "incentive to change" involves many of the wealthy people on this planet. Some of the worst communication skills I have observed come from extremely wealthy people. Many of them were not always rich, and actually demonstrated excellent communication skills while they were building wealth – but once they no longer needed anyone else on a regular basis in life, their skills diminished. Or, they simply chose not to use them. And, unfortunately, many begin to alienate friends and family. People only talk to them because they are rich – not because they want to.

I hope that people will talk to you because they wish to do so, and that you can help others to improve using these concepts. And, there is the power of

> *It is my wish that everyone will talk to you because they want to. It is my wish that you can use these principles to improve your relationships and your life with people who matter to you most.*

the pyramid. Once a few learn a skill they can train others. Then others can train others. This is called the Train the Trainer approach in business and has been used effectively for decades.

As I write this final chapter I think of the person seated to the left of me on the plane from Dallas to Atlanta last night. I was very tired and lucky enough to get an upgrade to business class after an 18-hour day… just about to fall asleep, the flight attendant came by to offer beverages and spoke to this lady first.

Not only did she treat him with respect, but she also demonstrated excellent skills at establishing the bridge and managing the traffic. It was a very short conversation, but I could tell that she had the skills.

She was reading a book, and at one point during the flight I asked her what she was reading. She told me it was a great book – and, that she liked finding little known authors just as much as reading the main stream best selling works. I couldn't resist. So, I told her that my book would be published soon, and after describing it, I got the same reaction that I have received hundreds of times. She said things like "That's so true! My friends talk about this all the time!"

It turns out that she is a very successful CEO of a company in Atlanta that specializes in offering unique "food-safe aluminum wares", all based on timeless design elements and hand-crafted by skilled artisans to independent specialty retailers" according to the website, Keanecompany.com.

In addition to finding a very successful niche, you will discover that the company believes in more than just profit and growth. I found the following on the site:

"We're especially proud to be partnering with an organization that plays such an active role in giving back to its community. Through a program administered by our factory, a primary school for nearly 600 children in the community in which our artisans live and work, provides a fully-paid education for local children, many of whom have parents that help to create our beautiful wares. From tuition to textbooks, all expenses are covered."

Wow. A company that understands the responsibility of giving back... a company that understands there is a balance between being successful and being responsible... a company that is not simply focused on the never-ending goal of more revenue and more profit, but that citizenship plays a vital role.

Congratulations, Kelie Kerns on being different. It's people like you who encouraged me to actually write down what I have been observing for years. Now, I just hope that others can use these concepts and share them with others. Time will tell.

If you don't have the incentive to change, think again – we all do.

Cheers, Brad Meisburg

APPENDIX

Conversation or Event Scorecard	Y/N	Supporting Evidence
Was the Relationship recognized?		Y if there was acknowledgement of Peer-to-Peer or Subordinate to Position of Authority
Was the Situation recognized?		Y if there was recognition of the correct situation: One-to-One, One-to-Few or One-to-Many
Was the Bridge Anchored?		Y if there were demonstrated techniques to keep the bridge or appropriate number of bridges anchored during the conversation
Was the Traffic Managed?		Y if there were demonstrated techniques to have a reasonable, appropriate balance in traffic flowing across the bridge or appropriate number of bridges
Was the Bridge closed appropriately?		Y if there were demonstrated techniques for good closure/next steps
Was there a Successful Outcome?		Y if there is evidence that the stated outcome was in fact achieved
Overall Score		Rate number of Y scores out of 6 possible and then select the result: **Not Successful, Moderately Successful or Successful**

Not Successful – There was not a successful outcome and one or more of the steps of the process need improvement.

Moderately Successful – There was a successful outcome, but one or more of the steps of the process need improvement.

Successful – There was a successful outcome, and all steps in the process were on track.

Examples of Supporting Evidence:

- Recognizing the Relationship – In the conversation, the individual clearly recognized that the situation was peer-to-peer or Subordinate-to-Position of Authority and initiated/maintained the conversation appropriately for the relationship.
- Recognizing the Situation – In the event, the individual clearly recognized that the situation was one-to-one, one-to-few or one-to-many and established the correct number of bridges so as to have a good balance with all participants.
- Anchoring the Bridge – In the conversation, the individual used appropriate techniques to make sure that the bridge or bridges were well anchored so that traffic could effectively flow and not get lost. If an anchor was weak or non-existent, the individual took appropriate steps to successfully re-establish the anchor.
- Managing Traffic – In the conversation, the individual demonstrated techniques to make sure that traffic was effectively flowing both ways with appropriate balance in the volume so that all parties feel good about the balance.

- Closing the Bridge – There was no abrupt ending to the conversation and/or event. Appropriate techniques were used to establish next steps or follow on conversations.
- Successful Outcome – The goals of the conversation or event were achieved. All parties feel good about the conversation.

Conversation or Event Scorecard	Y/N	Supporting Evidence
Was the Relationship recognized?		
Was the Situation recognized?		
Was the Bridge Anchored?		
Was the Traffic Managed?		
Was the Bridge closed appropriately?		
Was there a Successful Outcome?		
Overall Score		

PERSONAL ASSESSMENT SCORECARD	Y/N	SUPPORTING EVIDENCE
Are our conversations well balanced?		Y if the feedback is that most often the conversations are well balanced including good communications traffic in both directions – include examples if possible in supporting evidence. Otherwise, select N.
Do you feel that I have good listening skills?		Y if the feedback includes the perception that the individual listens well and shows good understanding and does not dominate conversations. Otherwise, select N.
Am I easy to talk to?		Y if the person giving feedback shares that the conversations are enjoyable and not challenging. Otherwise, select N.
Will improving my communication skills help with our relationship?		Y if the person giving feedback would like the individual to work on his or her communication skills. Otherwise, select N.

PERSONAL ASSESSMENT SCORECARD	Y/N	SUPPORTING EVIDENCE
Are our conversations well balanced?		
Do you feel that I have good listening skills?		
Am I easy to talk to?		
Will improving my communication skills help with our relationship?		

ACKNOWLEDGEMENTS

I wish to thank two wonderful editors, Marie Pettet and Jeff Ramminger, the design team at CreateSpace and many mentors over the years including Dr. John Blackburn, Dr. Steve Dyer, Dr. Lee Todd, Kerry Roller, Nick Mancini, Neal Elgersma, Paul Chermak, Gary Davis, John Maydonovitch, Dr. John Donovan, Glenn Osaka, Clark Straw, Jerry Tartaglia, Johnnie-Mike Irving, Kathy Boyd, Ray Arndt, Luigi Mantegazza, Debbie Dunnam, Deb Nelson, Ann Livermore, Paul Logue, Pat Adamiak, Uli Vandermeer, Sandeep Johri, Angela Cinefro, Brian Cohen, Brian Hill and Dr. Don Martin.

Finally, thank you to my friends and family for the encouragement over the years. Without you, this book would not have been possible.

INDEX

11094417R00096

Made in the USA
San Bernardino, CA
05 May 2014